Breach of Promise

Portraits of Poverty in North America

James A. "Gittings "

FRIENDSHIP PRESS • NEW YORK

Library of Congress Cataloging-in-Publication Data

Gittings, James A.
  Breach of promise: portraits of poverty in North America / James A. Gittings.

  ISBN 0-377-00181-3 (pbk.): $4.95
  1. Poor—United States. 2. Church work with the poor—United States. 3. Christianity and justice—United States. 4. Poor—Canada. 5. Church work with poor—Canada. 6. Christianity and justice—Canada. I. Title
HC110.P6G53 1988
362.5′575′0971—dc19   87-36769

Chapter 11 of this book is adapted from an article by James A. Gittings published in *Christianity and Crisis*, to which we are grateful for permission to reprint. Copyright February 2, 1987, *Christianity and Crisis*, 537 West 121st Street, New York, N.Y. 10027.

Unless otherwise stated, all Bible quotations in this book are from the Revised Standard Version, copyright 1946 and 1952 by the Division of Christian Education of the National Council of the Churches of Christ in the United States of America. Quotations have in certain instances been edited for inclusive language according to that organization's guidelines.

Except for the author, none of the people in the photographs in this book are the actual persons about whom the chapters are written.
Photo credits:
  Page 13: Martha Tabor/Impact Visuals, 1983
  Page 25: Steve Dunwell/Agricultural Missions
  Page 37: William Gillette
  Page 51: Paul Nonnast/Concern Magazine
  Page 75: Nancy Miller Elliott
  Page 103: Sara Krulwich/New York Times Pictures

ISBN 0-377-00181-3
Editorial Offices: 475 Riverside Drive, Room 772, New York, NY 10115
Distribution Offices: P.O. Box 37844, Cincinnati, OH 45237
Copyright © 1988 Friendship Press, Inc.
Printed in the United States of America

Acknowledgements

I owe this book to people who were willing to welcome me as a stranger, to eat with me, to tell me their stories. Even while the heart breaks over what these stories reveal about the breaking of covenants that should create community, healing begins to come when those who have most reason to turn away from an inquiring journalist extend their hands and confidences.

I want to thank the people at Friendship Press who have advised and worked on the manuscript of this book. Although I am leery of committees, I am grateful to members of the "Faces of Poverty" group who offered comments and suggestions, who had the kind of arguments with the text that I hope readers will have, and who helped provide for travel and research. In the end I found myself agreeing with all but one of their principal objections to my first draft. I am grateful also to my editors, who nagged at the writer and tugged at his words (as editors are wont to do) with good effect: editor Nadine Hundertmark who got the project under way with great patience and then left it to welcome her first child; interim editor Carol Ames who labored brilliantly over an erratic and difficult text, and provided the appendix. Special thanks are due as well to Mary Ellen Lloyd of the National Council of Churches Office of Domestic Hunger and Poverty, for encouragement at the book's most critical formative moment.

Without my wife, Sue, our children and other family members, without friends and deacons and good folk sung and unsung who were mediators of the grace that helped to keep the strands of my safety net strong enough to bear me up, this author would not be writing for this or any other audience. To all such, Peace, Thanks, and God Bless.

Stony Point, New York and Lincoln Park, New Jersey
1987

For Paul Lucia, faithful
in adversity, a friend
for the roads of winter

TABLE OF CONTENTS

Acknowledgements   iv

INTRODUCTION   *The Poor in the Land*   1

PART I   *Portraits of Poverty*   6
    Chapter 1   *Monongahela's Widow Jones*   7
    Chapter 2   *Joe Siranovitch Reflects*   11
    Chapter 3   *Racine Revisited*   16
    Chapter 4   *Molly's Salary*   22
    Chapter 5   *John and Jane Farmer Plant a Cross*   31
    Chapter 6   *A Hard Life in "The Corridor"*   41
    Chapter 7   *Falling Through the Net*   47
    Chapter 8   *A Criminal Dimension*   56
    Chapter 9   *The Lost Indian*   71

PART II   *Face to Face, Hand to Hand*   78
    Chapter 10 *What a Church Can Do*   79
    Chapter 11 *Straw for the Bricks of Brooklyn*   92

CONCLUSION   *Breach of Promise*   108
Appendix   122

Drawings on the facing page and elsewhere in this book are by Annie Q., an artist who uses her work to share the truths and gifts of people "from the streets" with the more "sheltered" community. She helps produce "Voices to and from the Streets," a newsletter published since 1982 for and by the homeless in New York City. With other artists she participates in workshops and shows that express the voices and visions of homeless people.

INTRODUCTION: The Poor in the Land

So if there is any encouragement in Christ, any incentive of love, any participation in the Spirit, any affection and sympathy, complete my joy by being of the same mind, having the same love, being in full accord and of one mind. Do nothing from selfishness or conceit, but in humility count others better than yourselves. Let each of you look not only to your own interests, but also to the interests of others. Have this mind among yourselves, which you have in Christ Jesus, who though being in the form of God, did not count equality with God a thing to be grasped, but emptied himself, taking the form of a servant. . . .

(Philippians 2:1-7)

This is a book about being poor in America. In this book we will examine many varieties of poverty and see the faces of many poor people. We will read about men and women who have been dispossessed and set adrift and about people who have lost the opportunity or capacity to earn a livelihood. We will read about people who have been denied some of their civil rights along with their bread. In one or two chapters, we will read about people who, at least temporarily, have lost a measure of their dignity as persons.

As we look at the experience of being poor in America, we will be searching out reasons for the conditions that make and keep people in economic poverty. We will discover, most of us not for the first time, that we do not have to travel far to find people in poverty: every congregation has several members or friends who are poor or near poverty. And so, in this book we will be trying to understand the best ways to help individuals known to us to change their situations and to salvage their dignity. At the same time we will try to discover how national or regional church groups can approach and help to change causes of poverty that are too powerful and complex for a single person or congregation to tackle alone.

As we read about people who are poor in North America, we will conscientiously work to avoid seeing them as a different species, inhabitants of a kind of sideshow featuring oddities outside the general run of humankind. Although none of us would deliberately create an "us and them" mentality with regard to people who are poor, our culture and media make it difficult to avoid focussing on "horror stories" instead of encountering real people. The ways that some individuals have chosen to relieve or struggle against the tedium of day-to-day poverty may appear eccentric to us. Or our own economic insecurities may lead us to accent differences between ourselves and the unemployed or dispossessed. But somehow, in this book, we must govern our imaginations and not let ourselves be sidetracked onto paths of sensationalism. In part, that has been my task as writer. It is also your responsibility as reader. To accomplish this, we shall draw our light from a source beyond the stories of the people in this book.

When we turn to that source, the Bible, we find that it allocates much attention and thousands of words to the sufferings of the poor. But it almost never places them—their thoughts, reactions and foibles—in the center of the narrative.* Instead, when the Scriptures introduce the subject of the poor—whether in story, law, prophecies, or parables—they almost always address the fortunate portion of humankind who are *not* poor. The biblical authors then ask or order that the prosperous set right the condition of poor persons, according respect to them. Frequently a warning is added to these exhortations: if you who are rich and powerful do not assist the poor, say the Scriptures again and again, thus-and-so will happen to you in this world and the next.

* In writing this book, I have tried to take an approach that I believe the Scriptures take: never to turn away from the hard questions that our subjects' situations will put to our more-or-less comfortable selves (I mean, of course, to myself as writer and to you as reader). Underlying this book, too, is the belief that the warnings the Scriptures utter are valid. As Christians understand it, justice is an objective rather than a subjective reality; God does not *will* to punish people, yet when we fail to keep God's covenant of justice, mercy and peace, justice will indeed "roll down like waters, and righteousness like an everlasting stream" (Amos 5:24).

Sometimes people who assert that justice both can and should be brought to bear on conditions that create poverty are discounted as "idealistic." Remarkable indeed would be a sixty-year-old journalist who could sustain idealism through a career in this century, nor have I been able to do so. But I do not think it idealistic to observe that people get into trouble when they break promises and fail to keep covenants. So *Breach of Promise* examines deep and powerful promises that are being broken every day with regard to the poor. To some extent, the covenants being broken are political ones, about which I will say more later. But predominantly the covenants that we break are religious. These covenants have been developed down a 2,500-year track from the vision of a human society whose creation God purposes, a vision which was held, with no apology for idealism, by the ancient Hebrews. Among them, Moses expressed the content of that early vision in speeches of farewell to his people.

Here is a passage from those speeches as they have come down to us in the book called Deuteronomy:

"At the end of every seven years you shall grant a release.

---

* The books of Job and Ruth are obvious exceptions to this generality.

And this is the manner of the release: all creditors shall release [forgo collection of] what they have lent to their neighbors; they shall not exact it of their neighbors, their kindred, because the Lord's release has been proclaimed. . . . But there will be no poor among you (for the Lord will bless you in the land which the Lord your God gives you for an inheritance to possess), if only you will obey the voice of the Lord your God, being careful to do all this commandment. . . ." (Deuteronomy 15:1-2, 4-5a)

"If there is among you a poor person, one of your kindred, in any of your towns within your land which the Lord your God gives you, you shall not harden your heart or shut your hand against your poor relative, but you shall open your hand, and lend the person sufficient for the need, whatever it may be. . . . If your relative, a Hebrew man, or a Hebrew woman, is sold to you, the person shall serve you six years, and in the seventh year you shall let the person go free from you. And when you let such people go, you shall not let them go empty-handed; you shall furnish them liberally out of your flock, out of your threshing floor, and out of your winepress; as the Lord your God has blessed you, you shall give to them. You shall remember that you were a slave in the land of Egypt, and the Lord your God redeemed you. (Deuteronomy 15:7-8, 12-15a)

The lovely dream of the Hebrews, a dream in which even the land was released from labor every seventh year (Leviticus 25:2-12), did not survive in practice. By Jeremiah's time, for example, Jews held other Jews in bondage (Jeremiah 34:8-17); and by Jesus' time automatic release from debts was so far from a reality that Jesus taught his followers to seek heavenly help in the matter (see the Lord's Prayer). Though the dream embodied in the covenant was not lived out, I have adopted as the guiding spirit of this book a section of Moses' speech as recorded in Deuteronomy. Here Moses imagines that his listeners have arrived at the eve of the seventh year, the year in which debts are to be forgiven. The old lawgiver further supposes that at such a time a poor person comes to a prosperous person for help. So Moses, who understands the human soul, instructs his listeners in advance:

"Take heed lest there be a base thought in your heart, and you say, 'The seventh year, the year of release is near,' and your eye be hostile to your poor kindred, and you give them nothing, and they cry to the Lord against you, and it be sin in you. You shall give to them freely, and your heart shall not be grudging when you give to them; because for this the Lord your God will bless you in all your work. . . . For the poor will never cease out of the land; therefore I command you, You shall open wide your hand to your kindred, to the needy and to the poor, in the land." (Deuteronomy 15:9-11)

Reduced to twentieth-century English, this mandate from Moses becomes direct, even earthy—and not at all idealistic. He tells the people to stop worrying about being repaid, to quit being selfish and to open their hands, because to be tight-fisted will "be sin in you" (and will bring that justice we have been talking about rolling down) and because to obey will mean that "the Lord your God will bless you in all your work." This all sounds very carrot-and-stickish, until we remember that Moses and the Hebrew people were engaged in forming a caring community whose immediate purpose was survival in the wilderness (the longer-term purpose was to serve as the demonstration project for God's gracious plan for all human communities). When we come to the Gospels, we find the idea expressed again with equal succinctness by Jesus. He said, "Save your life—and lose it; spend your life, and save it." It is, after all, the same thing.

Breach of Promise is *not* a book of numbers and statistics, although some will be found in the course of the chapters, and an appendix indicates sources for finding others. Statistics mean little until we know what they stand for. Far more important is meeting the people and communities to whose experiences we now turn, because from the biblical point of view we are taking, the people of this book have undeniable meaning and great value. That is why in certain chapters (as will be indicated) we have felt it necessary to protect the identities and sometimes the locations of some of the people we are about to encounter.

PART I: Portraits of Poverty

"How long will you judge unjustly
   and show partiality to the wicked?
Give justice to the weak and the fatherless;
   maintain the right of the afflicted and the destitute.
Rescue the weak and the needy;
   deliver them from the hand of the wicked."
Arise, O God, judge the earth;
   for to thee belong all the nations!
                    (Psalm 82:2-4, 8)

CHAPTER 1: Monongahela's Widow Jones

"You shall not pervert the justice due to the sojourner or to the fatherless, or take a widow's garment in pledge; but you shall remember that you were a slave in Egypt and the Lord your God redeemed you from there; therefore I command you to do this. When you reap your harvest in your field, and have forgotten a sheaf in the field, you shall not go back to get it; it shall be for the sojourner, the father-less, and the widow; that the Lord your God may bless you in all the work of your hands. When you beat your olive trees, you shall not go over the boughs again; it shall be for the sojourner, the fatherless, and the widow. When you gather the grapes of your vineyard, you shall not glean it afterward; it shall be for the sojourner, the fatherless, and the widow. You shall remember that you were a slave in Egypt; therefore I command you to do this." (Deuteronomy 24:17-22)

We want you to know, brothers and sisters, about the grace of God which has been shown in the churches of Macedonia, for in a severe test of affliction, their abundance of joy and their extreme poverty have overflowed in a wealth of liberality on their part. For they gave according to their means, as I can testify, and beyond their means, of their own free will, begging us earnestly for the favor of taking part in the relief of the saints. . . . (II Corinthians 8:1-4)

When the bulldozers, trucks, concrete mixers and laborers came up her road outside Monongahela, Pennsylvania, the Widow Jones watched them listlessly. And when they were gone, she was not surprised to see a sewage sludge treatment facility where a clump of box elders once stood at the turn of the road: it was just one more thing done to her without anybody asking first.

Margaret Hendricks Jones[*] was born forty-odd miles from Monongahela, just over the border in West Virginia. Her family brought her to Pennsylvania in 1939, just in time to meet and

---

[*] Not her real name; the town of Monongahela is an actual town near Margaret's village.

fall in love with Tommy Jones before he had to leave for a year of military training. For Tommy and Margaret one year of training stretched into almost six. Tommy spent them in the United States Army, and when the Army gave him back he had multiple (and poorly repaired) fractures of the legs, pelvis, chest and skull, courtesy of a rolling jeep on a Luxembourg mountain road. Margaret didn't care; she married Tommy anyway.

Tommy wasn't supposed to ever be able to work again: his disability was rated 90 percent. But he struggled, and Margaret prayed, and between the two of them they got him upright, and walking after a fashion, and even secured the promise of a job in a valley steel plant—if, the man said, Tommy had a way to get to work. A grateful country met this need by presenting the young veteran with an automobile fully equipped for a disabled man to drive. Which was wonderful, the couple agreed, until they later discovered that among the papers signed upon delivery of the car was a quitclaim for further disability claims of any kind against the government. The government's emissary in the matter, like many bureaucrats, had enlarged upon his mission in such a way as to protect his employer.

Nowadays a couple faced with such institutional self-serving would hasten to a lawyer to enter suit. Not Tommy and Margaret: they had had quite enough of Veterans Administration "services," and only wanted to start their life together. The only drawback was that Tommy's health remained fragile. There were many work days missed, and jobs involving even minimal lifting or carrying were barred to him. The steel company kept him on until it closed some twenty years later, but Tommy never made more than $8,000 in any year. At the end, under the strain of losing his employment, Tommy had a series of crippling heart attacks and almost died.

With Tommy unemployed, Margaret went to work. Her non-union job was on the cleaning crew of a hospital, which paid minimum wages. Somehow she and Tommy got by, assisted by the small earnings of their adolescent son, Tim. When Tim married, Margaret briefly despaired, but about that time the hospital staff organized a union, and wages began to climb. Thereafter she worked for fifteen years, her salary cresting at $16,000 in 1985.

Tommy's heart attacks changed his entire personality. He became moody, embittered, jealous of his wife and of his son. This jealousy manifested itself in sly suspicion, furious abuse, occasional violence. Margaret almost came to hate him. But then, like sun emerging from a cloud, Tommy changed again. The couple had two happy, cheerful years together. In the second of these two sunshine years, they decided to put a new roof on their house, incurring $12,000 of debt. Then Tommy died.

Margaret received the proceeds of Tommy's National Service life insurance policy. She promptly gave a large portion of it to Tim, who by now was married and had children but was jobless because of the flight of industry from the valley to the south and overseas. The balance of the insurance—$8,000—she placed in a savings account. It is an ordinary savings account, at an ordinary 5 percent interest, and one wonders about the morals of the banker who permitted her to settle for so little three years ago when the account was opened. In any case, Margaret receives about $440 a year from her insurance money. She also has Social Security—such an amount as a woman gets who never made more than $16,000 a year (and averaged much less), even in her final five years of work. On the total of the two sums she lives, faithfully paying off that $12,000 loan for the roof.

Margaret has no friends: "I'm not a joiner," she says. But she faithfully attends mass at the local Catholic church. And this year she sent a check to a radio evangelist "to help them widdas and orphans in Sudan." Otherwise, she spends her time polishing the tiny objects that abound in her little house, painting the frames of windows at the least show of wear, rearranging the photographs that line shelves and tables. She is sixty-five but acts much older.

The sludge treatment station has made her angry. "Me and Tommy were never busybodies," she says. "We weren't people to attend council meetings and stuff like that, making trouble. I never heard they was going to put that there until it happened. But that's the way the country is, isn't it? People who wouldn't put that thing next door to themselves will put it next to me and Tommy's house, the same way they put them halfway places and houses for dimwits next to the like of us but never beside themselves."

Margaret delivers this diatribe against the country's way of conducting social engineering in a room that displays Tommy's army discharge certificate in a gilt frame with a furled miniature flag across the top. The words she has spoken are vigorous in meaning, it occurs to me, but not in delivery: she is, as I said, listless.

As I leave her, I wonder how she gets by on her tiny income: I have not noticed a garden out back, and at the food store where I stop on the way out of town, prices are as high as those in

Pittsburgh. I also reflect on what a waste it is for a courageous and intelligent woman to seclude herself at so relatively young an age in four rooms crowded with memories, mostly bitter. There ought to be a group, I think to myself, that would come after her, and not take no for an answer, and get her out into the mainstream of life again.

Then I remember something she said: "Them girls I used to work with; they wanted me to go on a trip to Lancaster [about 140 miles away] this year. But when I got figgering, I couldn't afford it."

It occurs to me to wonder how much she has left over each month for gasoline just to make the trip downtown. And then I get to thinking how America treats the poor and old, by whom I mean anybody on a fixed pension or without a pension. Since the early seventies, by inflation and otherwise, we have picked them as clean as those chickens for sale in Margaret Jones' neighborhood store. In the United States, in 1985, the "poverty line" for a single person over sixty-five is set at $5,156 a year.[*] There is not much honor due a society that even pretends a person can live on so small a sum, or so I believe.

---

[*] Statistics Canada uses figures ranging from $7,568 to $10,233, depending on area, as "low income cutoffs" for "unattached" persons (single people in their own households). In 1985, just over 50 percent of elderly unattached women and 33 percent of elderly unattached men had incomes below these cutoff figures. See Appendix for more information.

CHAPTER 2: Joe Siranovich Reflects

> Come now, you rich, weep and howl for the miseries that
> are coming upon you. Your riches have rotted. . . . Your
> gold and silver have rusted. . . . You have laid up treasure
> for the last days. Behold, the wages of the laborers who mowed
> your fields, which you kept back by fraud, cry out. . . .
>
> (James 5:1-4)

Joe Siranovich* is a wonder. At sixty-three his brown hair is
unblemished by gray, and the skin of his forearms is taut over
smooth muscle. We have not met for thirty years, but he is openly
glad to see me. When he begins to talk, the thoughts that flow
outward in his pleasing baritone voice seem to replay for me an
internal conversation that has occurred many times before:

"You remember how it was. All along the rivers the towns were
self-contained, each one in its valley opening off the river, each
with its mill, its clubs, its high school, its football team. Well, it's
like somebody has wrote off those towns. Go up the Mon [the
Monongahela River in western Pennsylvania] and the mills is dead,
clean up to Elizabeth. Or up the Allegheny to Ford City: that's
all down too. Shut down. Then on the Ohio, there's Aliquippa—
shut down. The stuff up in Manchester—shut down. Steubenville—
might as well be shut down. The country has thrown away its
steel industry.

"There's a lot of new stuff going on. Labs, and engineering
companies, things like that there. But it isn't work for an ordinary
man. So around here, there's work if you got a college degree
in the right line. But there's nothin' for old people like me—the
traditional trades. Or for young people without an education. So
it isn't like a depression, where everybody's hurting a little bit.
Some people got it good. Real good and never better. And some
got it bad, all alone. By themselves.

"You got it wrong if you think me and Liz are poor. We got
a little more than $14,000 to live on, between Social Security and
my pension from the mill. 'Course, it don't go far, the way prices
are. But you know it's goin' to keep comin'. Or at least you *thought*

---

* Not his real name, although the towns mentioned are actual towns.

you knew it was goin' to keep comin'. . . .

"Did you hear that bunch in Texas is trying to cut our pensions? Pensions we earned a long time ago, pensions that was funded before this outfit bought the mill? Or, at least they told us it was funded. . . .

"I don't know if you know what happened out here. They kept saying these mills didn't make no money. But we made money every year. I hear they made money up there at Youngstown [Ohio], too. And there was supposed to be a lot of money layin' in the company.

"But that Texas bunch come in. First they bought Youngstown Sheet and Tube. It had money, Youngstown did. But not after that bunch had it for a while. Then they bought the place where I worked. And soon they was sayin' we were broke, too. Out here we know what happened. They wasn't steel men in Texas; they was bankers. Hasn't ever been a banker knew how to make steel.

"That stuff about foreign steel; it bothers me. I don't care how fancy you get, making things with plastics and aluminum and that kind of thing. When you come down to it, the *spine* of a big piece of machinery, or a building, or a tank, or a truck has got to be steel. And here's this big country of ours sayin' it doesn't want to make steel, it's going to import it. I can't see how that's good for national defense, to make yourself dependent on steel that's got to cross an ocean thousands of miles wide. Suppose there was a war? It ain't only steel that's gone. There's glass. And coal. And all the other things that went with that kind of business. Gulf Oil's left town too—gone to Texas.

"Like I said, it's like the country threw us all away, out here. But there's a lot more got thrown away: them clubs in our towns, they're closing. Some of the churches too. And all them little Jewish businesses: why, they used to call Charleroi 'Little Pittsburgh,' there was so many of them. Well, I was up there for a wedding not so long ago, and they ain't there now. The high schools are gone too—all put together twenty years ago, they were, in them jointures [union districts]. And even the fire companies, they're in trouble.

"Three things in my life I remember best of all. I remember the Depression: how hard it was for my dad bein' out of work, and for my mother. And I remember the war: I was two-and-a-half years over there, Infantry. And I remember going back to work when I got back. I worked hard—nobody can say I didn't give dollar's work for dollar's wage. But I didn't worry about the

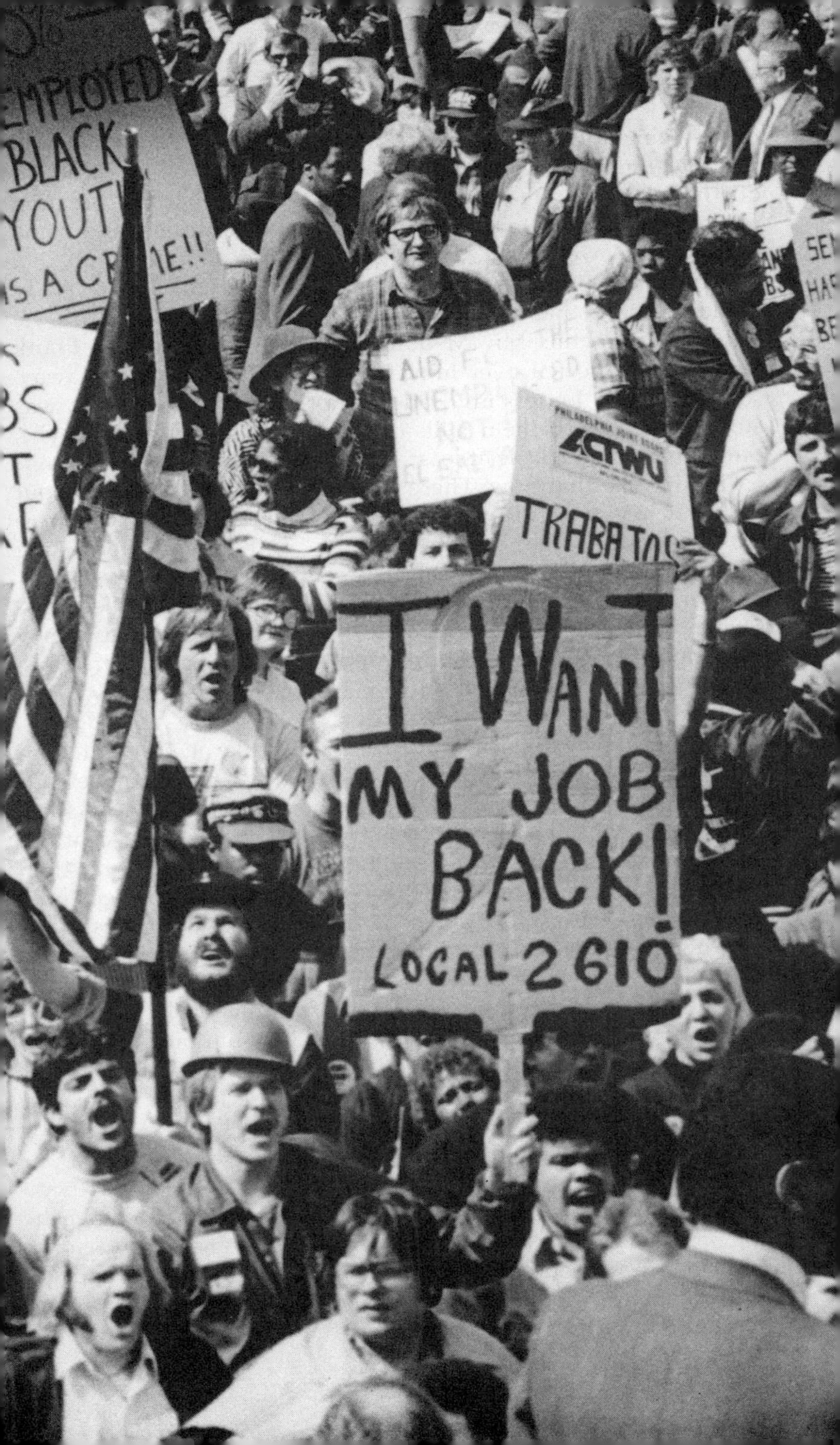
I WANT MY JOB BACK!
LOCAL 2610
ACTWU
BLACK

future: somehow I felt I'd *earned* a chance to work, over there in that Belgium mud. So I didn't save much: I always figured I'd do that the last fifteen years I worked. 'Cept that the inflation made it impossible to save out here in the seventies, and come the eighties—well, they let me go early and shut up shop. . . .

"My dad, during *his* Depression, used to talk about 'Andy Mellon.' About that big banker, like he *knew* him. Of course, he didn't know him: Mr. Mellon wouldn't have known Frank Siranovich if he fell over him. But he didn't seem so far away, somehow. And I guess my Dad musta thought Andy Mellon was suffering too, with them mills closed—not like we were, maybe, but embarrassed a little at least. Embarrassed.

"It isn't like that now. There isn't anybody embarrassed about us. We're just somethin' to be shut away out here. And I see where it's happening—what I knew was goin' to happen. After taking all that money out of here, and spreading it across the world— I swear it was our money that built those mills that killed us— Mellon Bank has lost a ton of money. When they kept that money here, and spent it building these mills, Mellon Bank didn't lose anything; why, it was the strongest bank in the country. Goes to show you. . . .

"They're trying to take this town and make it different than its soul—into little New York, maybe, with a lot of offices. Or maybe like that place in California where they make the chips. That's OK; we got to get ready, I guess, for the next century. But the way they did it: just pitching us out of work, and then messing around with our pensions: that isn't right. It used to be dirty out here with smoke and soot; there's different dirtiness now.

"Our kids, I worry about them. John has got his degree and will be OK. But Harry didn't want to study, he wanted to work. And he can't find anything steady. Liz and me, we'll be all right. We can't afford to do some stuff we talked about doing, but we've got our health. And this place. And if the country don't want us and our kind, well, we'll have to stay close to each other and the family until it's time to go.

"You asked me about the churches. There was a bishop of our church up in Youngstown, Bishop Malone, and he tried to do something to keep the mills open. But he couldn't, and then he got promoted, and went away. Up in Pittsburgh there was two outfits trying to do something. But one was Lutheran, and got into some stuff I didn't like—interrupting Sunday service at that rich church out in Shadyside. About the other one, I didn't hear nothing more after they first got started. I guess good times or bad times don't have anything to do with the churches anyway. . . .

"Good to see you, Jim. Do you remember Mel Cunir, that big tackle you guys had? Well, one day. . . ."

CHAPTER 3: Racine Revisited

And Jesus sat down opposite the treasury, and watched the multitude putting money into the treasury. Many rich people put in large sums. And a poor widow came, and put in two copper coins, which make a penny. And he called his disciples to him, and said to them, "Truly, I say to you, this poor widow has put in more than all those who are contributing to the treasury. For they all contributed out of their abundance; but she out of her poverty has put in everything she had, her whole living."

(Mark 12:41-44; see also Luke 21:1-4)

The author of the Gospel of Mark is thought to have written his book as a summary of the Apostle Peter's preaching and storytelling about Jesus. Luke is thought to have been a friend of Paul's and to have based his work on the teachings related by that great apostle to the Gentiles. Yet Luke quotes Jesus' words about the poor widow he observed in the temple in almost the same language that we see in the account from Mark. So we are perhaps entitled to think that the widow's face and gift must have burned their way into the mind of Jesus himself, just as the vigor of his remark impressed itself on the minds of the men and women who were closest to him.

Both Gospel writers position the account of the widow and her copper coins just after Jesus has ended a fierce denunciation of those who make a show of religion. The objects of his attack are people of learning and religious authority who expect the utmost deference as they go about their exercises of public piety. But these people are nonetheless tied to other practices by which, in one way or another, they take advantage of the poor. (Also see Matthew 23:1-33.)

After commenting on the widow's gift, Jesus goes on, as both Gospels recount, to relate a vision of coming upheavals and horrors in both natural and human spheres. Not only will the temple be destroyed, but a time of war, earthquake and famine will fall upon the world. This time of suffering will be the moment for the disciples "to bear testimony" (Luke 21:13) and by their endurance to gain their lives (v. 19).

In such a context, the widow's gift becomes a model of the sacrifice that may be required of every Christian. Her copper coins are worth more than greater sums because she has been unstinting, giving from her substance rather than from her surplus. So too, in their times of trouble, Christians are not to be concerned with saving anything of themselves—"Do not be anxious beforehand about what you will say, for it is not you who speak" (Mark 13:11)—but are to set themselves to "endure to the end." All other kinds of offerings, all other thoughts of eminence, are flimflam, because humankind, since the time of Abraham and Sarah, has been taught that "there are sacrifices which God does not ask, [but] there are none that a man or woman should not be willing to make."*

* * *

I thought of the "widow's mite" not long ago when I revisited, after a decade, the small town of Racine, West Virginia.† Although Racine is only 180 miles from the area of Pennsylvania where Margaret Jones and Joe Siranovitch live, it is a remote place. The town is situated south of Charleston at a point where, in narrow valleys, a small creek joins the Big Coal River. On the morning I arrived, the women of the local Church of God had set up a hot dog stand along the highway from which, via the CB radio in one husband's pickup truck, they were summoning truckers to swing by to purchase a benefit lunch.

The women at the hot dog stand on this pleasant May morning would not appreciate being labelled "poor." Indeed, by Racine standards, they are not poor. Attractively dressed in church-going outfits—and in considerable peril from splattering by the chili that makes "chilidogs" their most popular offering—the women are the Racine counterpart of the women's league of an upper-class suburb. Their husbands have jobs or have retired from jobs; they are the "prosperous" of their community.

But in talking with these women the relative nature of that prosperity becomes evident. One woman is agitated because her son has fallen in love with a girl whose parents "never had anything" and "don't amount to much." This woman is herself the wife of a retired miner, one of Racine's lucky ones whose service in the mines fell into time spans lengthy enough to qualify him for a pension. And all the women are angry this morning because

---

* *The Oxford Annotated Bible with the Apocrypha* (New York: Oxford University Press, 1965), p. 1513.
† Racine is an actual town in West Virginia.

the town's circulating library has been closed. "We're just hillbillies here," the most talkative of them observes, "and we're not supposed to be interested in books, I guess." Pressed for the reasons behind the closing, they say, "Times down here are bad and the state says it doesn't have the money. But you'd think they would cut something else back, not *this*."

A quick tour of Racine offers clues to its story. Immediately adjacent to the lot where the women have pitched their temporary hot dog stand is an attractive park developed with a considerable sum of state and federal money. In the park the usual variety of recreational activities are under way—Little League, picnicking and so forth. Around the bend the state has constructed a pleasant roadside park for highway travelers. At every crossroads stands a church. In town the established denominations have claimed their corners; outside of town are various chapels, holiness churches and an array of Baptists of several varieties. White paint peels from the planks of some church buildings, yet from one more well-to-do, strains of a nineteenth-century revival hymn spill across the valley from an expensive electronic amplification system.

Thus far, we might be anywhere in any of a dozen states of the U.S. Middle Atlantic or Upper South regions. But when we start to look at housing, the geography narrows. There are many empty dwellings. Most occupied houses are shabby and poorly constructed. Side roads and driveways are unpaved. Many gas stations, grocery stores and one-time specialty shops are locked up or abandoned. Traffic is light and—wonder of wonders—many people are walking or hitchhiking. The area, it quickly becomes clear, is very poor.

One can also see that this is an area where individualism runs rampant, even riot. The churches testify to that individualism; down this way they keep on inventing new denominations because the old ones just don't seem to fit. The few houses that are in good shape reveal the same inventiveness. One house in particular caught my eye. Ten years ago, when a friend occupied it, it was little more than a shack of boards nailed vertically to a frame, though age, simplicity of design and a lilac hedgerow lent it a certain grace. Since it has passed to a new owner, the house has sprouted turrets and a cupola, with the whole covered by cheap artificial brick siding. Like the hot dog stand, the electronic chimes and the community park, the house fairly shouts of aspiration, though it is aspiration straining, always, against limited funds.

Ten years ago when I came to Racine, most of the young people vere absent. They had left for Cleveland, Detroit, Cincinnati, altimore, even Washington, D.C., in search of jobs. Today young eople are to be seen in Racine again—not because there are jobs here, but because there aren't any jobs, at least not for people f limited technical or academic skills, in their onetime cities of efuge. So the young mostly "hang out": court each other, marry, ove into trailers, plant a garden if they can find space, raise hildren, live on income from part-time jobs and food stamps,[*] nd pop in and out of church in cycles, three years in, three years ut. The only major safety valve that really remains open is the rmy, so to the Army go considerable numbers of young men nd women.

A number of "teasers" keep Racine a homeplace despite the egion's drawbacks. One is the sheer beauty of these valleys, and heir variety. If one turn in the road reveals a huddle of poorly uilt homes, another displays a waterfall tumbling down the glen. n the woods, game and food and fuel are still to be found— esources not so abundant as they are farther north or south, erhaps, but known and available to local residents without much ass from landowners or state licensing officials. Then, too, rosperity still occasionally descends to these hills. Coal still lies bundant beneath the ridges, and from time to time some event a distant land makes it necessary to reopen the mines. Then he call goes out, the miners reappear to work for a decade or o, and car dealers flourish once more.

But none of this is within local control. When power companies urned to constructing atomic plants, they also bought up the oal fields. Thus coal, with its temporary (and to some extent emediable) residues of ash and sulphurous waste, is not permitted o compete in the United States with atomic power, with its otentially permanent hazards to health and environment. So a oom in the coal fields is nowadays almost always the result of decision to export coal. But most of the time, coal miners just ream of a day when somebody will consider their region and heir skills to be important again.

With the major coal operations shut down, the poor grow poorer. hey can't even take axe and saw out to cut wood for building r repairing homes anymore. The woodlands have been sold for acation homes; the new owners don't object if you gather fallen

---

In the U.S., 19 million people use food stamps; 35 million have incomes low nough to make them eligible for this program.

timber for firewood, but they'll have the law on you for theft of standing trees. And as old skills are lost, the house trailer, ever third- or fourth-hand, is the shelter of preference for young families. (Like the houses, the trailers also have ways of sprouting wings and ells as the number of people around the supper table grows.) The state has attempted to provide some low-income housing, but its limited funds are being cut back; next to no low-income housing has been built in the U.S. in the 1980s.

West Virginians around Racine are conscious of receiving the short end of the American stick. Pockets of political radicalism exist, astonishing in the ferocity with which they regard the "owners" of their state. Some of these small circles of dissent derive from outlanders who have settled in the region. A man named Golden, for example, lived near Racine for many years and taught the few who would listen a primitive form of Marxism. He is still remembered for the "primal scream" he launched down the valley every evening! But for most people, the feeling of being abused grows from the reality of having been left out of jobs and prosperity. People around Racine don't know why there are so few factories, why mining is so sporadic, or why so little new industry appears. They do understand, however, that park the state and federal money built. One woman says, "It don't change anything, but it made somebody feel better."

Yet the women of the Church of God run their hot dog sale. And up the road in an old post office, a used clothing store has opened; "Any item, ten cents," reads the sign. This little service enterprise, the brainchild of a Racine woman, draws its supplies from the closets of the area's more prosperous citizens and those of the more affluent community to the north, in Charleston. Elsewhere, there is a good food pantry, locally supported. And scout troops. And deacons' funds. And so on, until it is apparent that the small part of the area's population that is reasonably well-off is doing, or trying to do, what larger groups of their kind do anywhere in North America. The trouble is that no big pools of developmental or charitable capital are available to them, and that their burden, in terms of the percentage of the population in need, is greater than that borne elsewhere.

Even so, two elements in local society almost redeem the situation. One is the extended family: Racine is still a place where Uncle Bob lives up around the bend and Aunt Sally just over the hill. Families help each other; plenty of people are improperly fed, but few are hungry. The other kind of help goes beyond the family. It is the habit that poor people seem to have, wherever the ties of community still exist, of helping one another. Back at the hot dog stand, the wife of the retired miner complained of a nephew: "He don't make but a few hundreds a month, and on the way home from getting paid, he'll loan half of that out."

Just so: among decent people who are poor, one always has "ten for a friend." That generosity surely can be emulated by more prosperous people everywhere (as it could have been in Jesus' day). But the generosity of neighbors cannot mask the fact that the people of Racine, after a hundred years of on-again, off-again work, are a defeated people. The high per capita crime rate, the incidents of domestic neglect or abuse, the widespread use of alcohol to blunt the edge of misfortune and the poor health that afflicts so many of the young and old—all combine to make Racine an unhappy place.

While I was in a Racine grocery store, an old woman put down her purse. In an instant, it was gone. Everyone gathered around the distraught woman, who had just lost the cash from her welfare check. Expressions of comfort came from all sides, even as all darted glances of suspicion at one another. The incident seemed especially sad to me because I knew from my visit that the people of Racine have tried hard to be caring and supportive to one another during long years of trouble. They have indeed, like the woman in the temple, tried to give unstintingly from limited resources. After all their effort, it is a shame to see them denied—by such an incident in the community and by hundreds of decisions made by those outside the valley—the chance to feel altogether good about themselves.

CHAPTER 4: Molly's Salary

So if there is any encouragement in Christ, any incentive of love, any participation in the Spirit, any affection and sympathy, complete my joy by being of the same mind, having the same love, being in full accord and of one mind. Do nothing from selfishness or conceit, but in humility count others better than yourselves. Let each of you look not only to your own interests, but also to the interests of others.
   (Philippians 2:1-4)

And Zaccheus stood and said to the Lord, "Behold, Lord, the half of my goods I give to the poor; and if I have defrauded any one of anything, I restore it fourfold." And Jesus said to him, "Today salvation has come to this house, since he also is a descendant of Abraham." (Luke 19:8-9)

Give alms from your possessions to all who live uprightly and do not let your eye begrudge the gift when you make it. Do not turn your face away from any poor person, and the face of God will not be turned away from you. If you have many possessions, make your gift from them in proportion; if few, do not be afraid to give according to the little you have. So you will be laying up a good treasure against the day of necessity. For charity delivers from death and keeps you from entering the darkness; and for all who practice it charity is an excellent offering in the presence of the Most High. (Tobit 4:7-10*)

It is not true, as some think, that the rich are cursed in the New Testament. Jesus' comparison of a rich person to a camel trying to pass through the eye of a needle (Matthew 19:24), the harrowing story of Lazarus begging at the rich man's gate (Luke 16:19-31), even the parable of the rich farmer who built barns to store surplus crops (Luke 12:16-21) are not so much condemnations as warnings against dangers that attend the accumulation and possession of money. Chief of these hazards are covetousness and that arrogance that will not depend on God for entrance to the kingdom (see

---
* The Book of Tobit is in the Apocrypha.

what Jesus says about the poor and the rich in Luke 6:20-36).

In biblical terms, a rich person's sense of true humility is demonstrated by showing mercy and giving alms. Indeed, "alms" derives from the Greek *eleemosyne*, "pity." A modern dictionary defines almsgiving as the act of "giving something (as money or food) freely to the poor." What troubles us in putting that definition into practice is the adverb "freely." Many modern North Americans are embarrassed by the presence among us of people who need to ask for help. They and their situations give the lie to elements of our national myth (and even to a version of a widespread religious ethic), which holds that anyone who works hard can make it here (and that God blesses those who do).

Sometimes, in order to avoid that embarrassment about the poor, we turn to established institutions that will disburse the alms on our behalf. But these institutions and agencies were not created to keep us from having to give in person, but because none of us alone can give what is needed on the necessary scale. Many of us continue to look for personal ways to give, and often find those ways through working with social service agencies, whether those connected with churches or others. In some small communities we can still see how alms were given in the decades before the majority of our countries' people clustered in urban areas, where the need for service agencies grew with the population.

* * *

I found such a community in eastern North Carolina. It is a tiny place of perhaps two thousand people, half of them black. If what follows flatters the people of the community, remember that the town is no paradise. Twenty-four years ago, on my last visit, the white residents were engaged in bitter resistance to the expansion of voting rights for black residents, and open occupancy in housing had not been dreamed of. Today the town is still not a place where a young black male should attract much attention by force of personality, ambition or talent, for the white population continues to mutter about the "place" of "our Negroes." Yet the town is also home to an eighty-six-year-old black woman named Mary Longacre Platt.* Called "Molly" by everyone, she lives by herself in a tumbledown house on an unpaved street beside the graveyard that once marked the town's western border. I suggest

---

* This is not her real name, nor is Edgerton the real name of this North Carolina town.

that the town—I'll call it Edgerton—merits a considerable measure of forgiveness for past sins by its care and concern for Molly Platt.

Despite the sound of her middle name, Molly never married, though for sixteen years she raised a sister's boy, who left for New York one day and was never heard from again. Nor did Molly ever have a job of the sort that pays into Social Security and provides hospitalization. She spent her active life cleaning and "doing for" two families in the town. The families are not rich: one has always earned its income from the town's only insurance agency, the other (when Molly worked for them), from the earnings of a salesman for the Sunshine Biscuit Company.

Mary Longacre Platt's family and friends are all dead. Gone, too, are her employers. The women of the Philathea Class at her church have also "crossed over," as Molly says, and their grand-daughters sit in their places. As far as natural ties are concerned, the old woman is alone.

Apparently Molly Platt has always been one of those people who attract attention, speculation and concern without ever meaning to do so. Since she is obviously a quiet person, not in the least flamboyant, it was not easy to discover why. Two reasons have turned up. First, Molly walked each day (until two years ago, when her legs gave out) to a grocery store in the center of town. Used to seeing the aged lady walking, people took to stopping to offer her a ride. For each who stopped, Molly had the same reply: "Ah'd druther walk, thanks, but"—and here her smile broke out wide as heaven's gate—"God loves you foh askin'." That smile became a town institution, a treasure; people continued to stop just to receive it.

The second reason dates from a custom practiced by the women of the Philathea Class. Each year they drew names to select their "Sunshine Sisters." To one's Sunshine Sister one sent a birthday card and, as family occasions demanded, a card of sympathy or congratulations. Molly Platt found the tradition meaningful and took her responsibility seriously, including the rule that recipients never learn their Sunshine Sister's identity.

When Molly turned sixty-eight and her two employers told her that she "need not come in again to clean" (her limited strength having made her work ever harder for her), she searched for something to do. The custom from the Bible class suggested itself to her, and for many years thereafter the people of the town received hand-drawn cards of sympathy or congratulation from an unknown person who signed herself "Sunshine Sister." These

"cards"—often folded sheets of tablet paper—were distinguished by atrocious spelling errors and loving simplicity of thought. Thus, a card received by the wife of the town's agricultural agent on her husband's death:

> You done all thet you coulde to mek him happee but now Jesus done got the job an he goin todo it so good you be happee when you see. so Rest Easy. You Cry, thet's al right, but you a good womin and you goin be happy agin. your Sunshine sister.

These messages became collectors' items in town. The mystery of their source added to the piquancy. Then Molly's legs gave out and she could no longer walk to the post office. One day she asked a neighbor to mail a letter for her. The neighbor, who had once received a "Sunshine Letter" herself, recognized the handwriting and told the folks at church. Soon the secret was out all over town; the community's "Sunshine Sister" was that lady out by the edge of the graveyard, the one with the smile and the blessing.

Perhaps that's why Edgerton has taken unusually good care of Molly Longacre Platt. It was to be expected that the women who originally employed her saw to it during their lifetimes that their faithful retainer received a little money each month in her old age; one can even understand why their daughters might continue the custom. But when the granddaughters of the original employers continue to stop by once a month to give Molly her "salary," we have clearly passed from the realm of custom to that of virtue.

Asked to post a letter one day, the woman who lives next door to Molly made a point of not noticing that no money for a stamp was offered. Nor has she "noticed" the omission at any time in the years that have followed. In addition, this neighbor similarly ignores the absence of money on occasions when Molly asks her to "pick up a quart of milk while you're at the stoh." A day or so after Molly's "salary" is delivered, the woman next door shops extensively for her and, of course, is reimbursed. But over the course of a month the neighbor, out of her own slender resources, may pump twenty dollars into Molly Platt's kitchen—always being careful "not to notice."

Joe Carter, down the street, "stops by" Molly Platt's house almost every day, "just to say hello"—and just happens to carry some wood in "to help Miz Platt to do her cookin'." In late spring, Joe drops by with spade and cultivator to "get you your garden ready for planting, Miz Platt, so's you can put them tomatoes in." Somehow he always has some extra seed and some plants to be put in. And, in long midsummer evenings, Joe and his boy "stop by" regularly, to "chop them weeds a bit, Miz Platt—we got the time." In July when Joe drops in, Molly proudly gestures toward a chip basket. "They's some tomatoes there for you, Joe; I expect yo family'll like the taste." And Joe, who has tomatoes to spare from his own garden, thanks Miz Molly kindly.

Every other day the township sheriff's car stops by Molly Platt's door. Once that car wouldn't have been welcome; would in fact have caused fear. But the boy who got into trouble so often, so long ago, is gone now. And time softens the edges of everything, even fear, when one is old. The cop comes, in fact, to check on Molly's health and safety out of his own desire to do so, and because she has become an institution in the town. But the occasion, both realize, must be made personal. He is appropriately grateful for that cup of coffee, and finds it "maghty fine."

Coordinator for much of this attention is Molly Platt's pastor. He has made sure that this older member is not forgotten: a deacon calls to bring her to the A.M.E. (African Methodist Episcopal) Church every Sunday and, when she wants to come, on Wednesday nights for prayer meeting. He reminds the women's association not only to include her in every potluck dinner and social event, but to invite her to help in the preparation as well. The pastor is also the architect of Molly's "arrangement" with the black undertaker in the county seat, an arrangement much spoken of around Edgerton.

When Molly was seventy-two, she began to worry about death— not about dying, but about death and, specifically, about who would bury her and pay for the burial. She asked her pastor to ask the undertaker to call on her, and when he came, she asked if there was anything she could do for him that would pay for her funeral ahead of time. "I got no money," she told him, "but I got these two hands." Nonplussed, the undertaker asked for time to think about the matter and promptly beat it back to see the pastor. Between them, they came up with a "job" for Molly.

Molly's job was to staple palm-paper hearts to cleft pieces of wood to form the familiar undertaker's fan once found in every funeral parlor in the U.S. "You do me a hundred o' them every month, Molly, and I'll give you a credit of two and a half cents each. Now you are goin' to live a long time yet, I know. By the time you die, there is goin' to be enough money in that account for me and the pastor to bury you." So saying, the undertaker left, and within a few days a large cardboard box was delivered, containing preprinted paper and sticks. Once a month either the pastor or the undertaker picks up Molly's hundred fans. Neither mentions that the funeral parlor was air-conditioned a decade ago and that a closet in the church is slowly filling up with Molly's prepayments.

There is much I could not find out about Edgerton's care for Molly Platt, including who pays for her electricity or the source of a third monthly envelope beyond those two "salaries." I *did* discover why her property has not been seized for taxes: "Hey, man, we can wait for that old lady to die; we're waiting for a lot of people in this county," says the clerk. One admires the clerk's sense of proper time, and wishes more clerks like this one were tucked away in North American tax offices.

Despite the kindness with which Molly Platt is surrounded, Edgerton is full of evidences that the old woman had better hurry up and die. Halfway between Edgerton and a neighboring community a small shopping center is under construction; it almost certainly signals the end for Edgerton's own handful of stores, completing the erosion of community self-consciousness that began years ago when area school districts were consolidated. Molly's beloved A.M.E. Church is also moving. The prosperity of its members has enabled the congregation to purchase property on the other edge of town, and soon a new building will be constructed. A state training school under construction will bring new families to the area, so the town will grow in size and complexity. Soon the concern that is now shown personally will give way to a "community services" approach.

* * *

Perhaps now, before Molly "crosses over" and the community adopts the "improved" ways of doing things involved in United Ways and family service bureaus, it will be profitable to look at some elements of Mary Longacre Platt's home-grown "retirement." We can begin with the clubbishness of the effort: a group of citizens, white and black, decided that this woman was not going to want for life's necessities. Each person made the decision individually, it is true, but they soon discovered one another and thereafter coordinated their efforts when necessary.

Further, they permitted Molly Platt to live with the myth of entitlement. That was a *salary* that was delivered by each of her two families; the basket of tomatoes given by Molly to Joe was a "gift" and was gratefully received. In her own way, Molly's neighbor also honored the concept, by "not noticing" about money, and the circle at church, by asking her to come early to wipe the stainless steel silverware for the covered-dish supper, manifested a similar care for her integrity. Even the cop, checking on her safety, cheerfully underwent the ordeal of drinking Molly's execrable coffee for the sake of reciprocal kindness.

Concerning this communal support of an old woman's sense of self-worth two things can be said. First, in the scheme of things in an old-style southern community, that sense of self-worth, of making a contribution, has a historical foundation. Two families of modest means were enabled by a younger Molly's help to live like gentry, clearly feeding *their* sense of self-worth. They owe her a great deal that cannot be paid in coin of the realm because hers was a character-forming, not just a labor-saving, contribution. Second, even in later years Molly's contribution to the town was not insignificant. Without urban civic achievements to boast of, small towns like Edgerton must create their own local myths. Chief among these myths is one that begins "Folks around here are friendly; they take care of each other, why, just look at that. . . ." And "that," when explained, turns out to be someone like Molly whom everyone looks after. (Of course, all such beneficial myths have their underside as well: those in equal need who are never mentioned to strangers because the people of the community pretend not to see them.)

But we cannot leave Edgerton without also asking why Molly's need for that sense of entitlement exists, and what it is in members of small communities that enables them so clearly to sense, and to act on, that need.

My answer is not profound. In nature, one gives to infant creatures; all others must forage for themselves. To be able only to receive is to be relegated to incompetency unless one is permitted the reality, or the illusion, of drawing upon an earned or future credit. Mary Longacre Platt will go to her grave with a sweetness in her face because she has received such credit for her self-worth and community contribution. At any point that sweetness might have been soured—by a neighbor unwilling to run errands, a laborer "too tired" to keep in touch with her, an undertaker less sensitive to her pride, a set of granddaughters too selfish to "look out for that old black lady who used to help

Grandma." None of these things happened—in Molly's case.

Somehow the machinery by which people in larger communities give their alms has got to be oiled once more—redeemed, really—with the sensitivity to self-worth and entitlement that has infused the efforts to help Molly. That's Edgerton's lesson for most of the rest of us. But the people in our countries' Edgertons likewise have to understand that it is vastly easier to care for a Mary Longacre Platt in a town of two thousand than it is to care for fifty thousand Mollys who are hidden in block after dreary block of substandard housing in a metropolis. And the people of Edgerton—as well as the rest of us—have got to achieve this understanding, because it is partly in response to our calls for economy in government and for reductions in welfare payments and services that the little humanity that was once found in our state, county or provincial welfare systems has been extinguished by a harried bureaucracy forced to count its pennies.

CHAPTER 5: John and Jane Farmer Plant a Cross

"And if you will obey my commandments which I command you this day, to love the Lord your God, and to serve God with all your heart and with all your soul, God will give the rain for your land in its season, the early rain and the later rain, that you may gather in your grain and your wine and your oil. . . . Take heed lest your heart be deceived, and you turn aside and serve other gods and worship them, and the anger of the Lord be kindled against you, and the Lord shut up the heavens, so that there be no rain, and the land yield no fruit, and you perish quickly off the good land which the Lord gives you." (Deuteronomy 11:13-17)

"But none can enter the house of the strong and plunder their goods, without first binding them; then indeed they may plunder the house." (Mark 3:27)

Something about land—the tilling of it and the harvesting of it—has always instilled in farmers an awareness of God and God's mercies. Some of the most dramatic speakers for God, from Amos to Peter Marshall, seem to have come to the city from the country.

At the same time that working the land produces one kind of God-centeredness, pride in the land and what it produces can also lead to pride in oneself as the producer. Some have labeled as "provincialism" a tendency to focus on the land and on those who produce its good fruits. To me it comes across as the countryside's own brand of pride, by which farmers regard themselves and their families as more virtuous and hard-working than others. Of course, this pride leads, as all pride does, to judgments expressed about those who live in other ways. I still remember some judgments expressed twenty years ago when the church was pressing for extended welfare rights for unemployed urban black people. Letters from midwestern farmers to the denominational magazine where I worked insisted that these unemployed people must have something wrong with them. Otherwise, the writers insisted, they would find a way to get off the dole. It did not occur to the farmers that in many cases jobs for these unemployed black people did not exist.

The decades from 1940 to 1980 were fairly good times on the farm. If one worked hard, established favorable banking and credit relationships, and kept up with both markets and improved agricultural techniques, one could hope not only to make a good living but also to expand the family enterprise. Some farmers became "rich"—a word they use themselves—and if their wealth existed mostly on paper as land and equipment and livestock futures, there often was still enough cash in the bank to permit mid-winter trips to Florida or Arizona sunshine, with a bit left over for flying lessons or a down payment on a Piper Cub. Toward the end of this era, the magic word "leverage" was uttered in "Ag" classes at the university and in the roadside cafes where farmers gathered for coffee. "Leverage" involved taking advantage of high land values and low interest rates to pry loose large sums in loans from banks and other credit sources in order to expand family acreage and buy costly machines. In the background, justifying such risk-taking, were ever-increasing export markets for corn, wheat, soy beans, and sometimes meat. Almost everywhere the best and most progressive farmers fell into the trap, mortgaging their fields to the hilt. By 1986, U.S. farm debt stood at $215 billion and was concentrated in middle-size farm operations—primarily the family farm. Farm debts in Canada are similarly high.

We all know some of what happened. Overseas markets proved unpredictable, drying up as a result sometimes of good harvests in the USSR and China, sometimes of Argentine or Australian competition, sometimes of political tensions, sometimes of over-pricing. Costs of equipment and operations soared. Above all, a new U.S. fiscal policy, designed to "damp down" inflation even as it attempted to restore the price-competitiveness of American products, led to falling farm prices, rising interest rates (they later eased a little, but too late for most farmers) and falling land values. (In Canada, farm land values are stable at best.) Thus, a national decision made to benefit all citizens brought disadvantage to a part of the people, the farmers.

Now the fruits of "leveraging" ripened, and bitter was the eating. Declining property values destroyed the security that backed the omnipresent loans. Stationary or falling crop prices meant that income failed to keep up with rising production costs. Above all, soaring interest rates meant that the proportion of farm income required to service past debts climbed ever higher. For many a farmer, a day came when, approaching the bank for crop loans, he or she was told that the farm balance sheet indicated that no more of that magical "leverage" existed and that no loan for seed or fertilizer or feeder-beef would be forthcoming.

Now farmers have learned what it is to be captive, like urban blacks or New England shoemakers, to economic decisions and import trade-offs beyond their control. But the farmers' psychological pain may be more intense—at least farmers think so—because: (1) farmers have had no experience with economic collapse since the Dust-Bowl days of the 1930s; (2) the solitary nature of farming provides no company in times of difficulty; and (3) the farmer's sense of closeness to God and to nature during the good times makes him or her feel especially abandoned by the Lord in the bad times and, sharing the perspective of the historian of Deuteronomy, perhaps even under punishment at God's hands.

In Iowa, Kansas and Nebraska the disaster has been felt by great numbers of people. Land values have fallen, sometimes by two-thirds. Mortgages have been and are still being cancelled. Notes are called due, properties seized. Every county has its parade of farm equipment sales. Lifestyles that for decades had approached opulence have suddenly started to shrivel toward hardscrabble levels. Such suffering has occurred across the Midwestern farm belt and in other parts of the country as well as in Canada. In the southern U.S. states, farms operated by blacks have almost disappeared; farmland owned by black farmers is being lost at a rate of 9,000 acres a week.

Most farmers handle their distress with great fortitude. But there are others who, by circumstance, weakness, exceptionally bad luck or official mistreatment, have been driven to violence. A rural society proud of its morals and kindness has begun to record more cases of wife and child abuse, drunkenness, divorce, suicide and murder. Through it all, like almost everyone stricken by economic misfortune, farmers have had to endure a steady erosion of their sense of pride and self-respect.

* * *

The town of Allerton (population 650) in Wayne County, Iowa, has shared in this rural tragedy. Its three banks have all but shut down their agricultural loan operations, and five of the seven farmers who belonged to the tiny (eighty-one member) Allerton Community Church have gone out of business.

The scene for change in Allerton is set at 8:30 on an October

morning five years ago. On the Brill farm, Blanche Brill knows
something is wrong.* Her husband, Joe, has made his customary
return to the house after the morning feeding chores to share
a cup of coffee with her. He has just emptied his cup but shows
no disposition to return to the feedlot. "What's wrong, Joe?"
Blanche asks. And Joe, who has not wept in front of his wife in
thirty years of marriage, puts his head down on the table and
sobs. In four minutes Blanche is sobbing too, for Joe has just told
her—bolt from the blue—that they will lose the farm.

How could it be that a wife would learn of such a threat so
abruptly?

The trouble with many farmers, as they will tell you themselves,
is that they find it difficult to talk over their fears and dis-
appointments. A typical male farmer will withhold bad news from
his wife as long as he can. When he is finally driven to inform
her that the bank is pressing for overdue payments or that he
cannot obtain a crop loan, the couple then conspires to keep the
unpleasant news from their children. And the children, when they
finally learn the extent of the trouble, will be sworn to conceal
the family's hardships from other children at school. Despite the
talk of how "everybody is friendly out here," community mores
contain a strong streak of privatism. The rural Midwestern male
ethos provides for a warm greeting, a slap on the back, and a
"don't tell me your troubles." Above all, prevailing opinion holds,
one must say nothing about family difficulties to one's pastor.

Blanche Brill was appalled that morning to discover that a hearing
on foreclosure on their property would be held the next week.
Yet in one way she was relieved. Joe had been so *strange* lately.
He had continually snapped at Billy, their good-natured, seldom-
offending teenager. He had shouted at her in a way he had never
done in all their years of marriage. He had started to drink, to
smoke heavily, to go off by himself in the family car for hours
on end. Now at least she had a reason, one she could deal with,
if Joe would just stop crying. And when he did not stop, Blanche
did the unthinkable: she called the minister.

Her call was the first good thing to happen to the Brill family
that autumn of 1983. When Pastor Ross Blount got to the Brill
farm that Saturday morning, Blanche was direct. "I'm afraid that
Joe is getting sick or something. Sick in the head." Ross Blount

---

* Allerton is an actual community, but Brill is not the real name of this Allerton
family.

heard that statement against a background of dealing with people under strain that stretched from his Peace Corps days in Nigeria through six years of ministry in Appalachia to his own seven years on an Allerton farm. He listened, then went home to talk with his wife, Lorena. And she, with the women of the three weekly prayer groups she leads, promptly called for a community day of prayer for the farm crisis. The Day of Prayer became a landmark in all that followed, for it marked the beginning of something new in Allerton: a sense of unity with neighbors in their difficulties.

To the hearing on the Brill foreclosure came the people of the town, led by Pastor Blount. They appeared in their best clothes and most decorous behavior. They did *not* save the Brill farm. They did, however, plant a cross on the courthouse lawn, amid a blaze of sun glinting off the T.V. camera lenses. The cross symbolized many things: a sense of loss at the demise of one more family farm, a sense of solidarity with the dispossessed family and, as any cross must, an expectation of change. But as the Allerton cross was seen on television screens across the nation, it brought home to the American people the knowledge that something tragic, something harmful, was happening on the plains.

Not long after the hearing, the churches of Iowa organized a conference in Des Moines on the farm crisis. Joe Brill couldn't go; he had another hearing to face. So Ross Blount asked another farmer from the congregation to attend. Ross suspected that this young farmer was in economic trouble, too.

At the conference Kate Simon, pastor of a church not far from Allerton, was among those who spoke. Kate told the story of farm tragedy in her parish. She told of efforts by farmers to "beat" the sales of seized machinery by conspiring to underbid on behalf of the defaulters. She told of organizing and sending delegations to visit banks, state officials, the federal government. She told how farmers were discovering one another, joining together to search for collective ways out of difficulty. And she told her listeners that the church simply must find ways of standing with and serving its increasingly desperate constituency.

Kate was not telling success stories. No changes had resulted from the efforts she described. But throughout her remarks, Blount recalls, the young clergywoman projected immense concern and caring, and a sense of great energies already expended for farmers on the edge of ruin. Sensing a stirring on his right, Blount looked toward the young farmer who had come with him. "He was wiped out by what had been said," the pastor remembers, "but he was liberated too. On the way back he found himself able to talk about his problems. And he told me that until Kate Simon spoke, he really didn't think anybody cared what was happening to people like him. So together, driving home, we talked about what our church could do."

Ross Blount is a graduate in agriculture of Iowa State University and the proprietor of a 270-acre farm that has been in his wife's family for three generations. He is also pastor of the Garden Grove Community Church (20 members, United Methodist and Presbyterian) and of the Allerton Community Church (81 members, Presbyterian). Lorena Blount is a teacher at nearby Indian Hills Community College. Deeply rooted in the Allerton community, the two are respected and trusted.

Ross and Lorena, together with Joe Brill and the young man who went to Des Moines, sat down to plan a role for the church. "What we were trying to do was to find ways to understand what was happening," Ross remembers, "and it took a while. At first it never occurred to us that the change in monetary policy in Washington had anything to do with what was happening here."

Lorena and the women of the prayer groups may have unintentionally struck the note that opened the community to change. While using a Bible study on the Minor Prophets from *Concern Magazine*, they came upon the line, "The women of my people you drive out from their pleasant houses" (Micah 2:9). One of the group cried out, "It's happening to me!" From that moment of uncovered grief, the women decided to stand together, to share completely in one another's woes. They decided, Ross says, "to be indeed servants of the Word," learning "from their own hurts and from the hurts of others." It was the community's women, through the Bible clubs, who effectively stripped the masks of secrecy from familial tragedies.

Within weeks a small band of farmers and their pastor had energized the community. A Men's Bible Club, the first in years, was formed. Packets of materials on the farm crisis were distributed throughout the community. Local people were put in touch with legal service groups like the Prairie Fire organization. A county-wide Farmers' Survival Committee was formed. Counseling networks among peer groups were started, as well as emergency services for family crisis counseling, spouse abuse and child abuse. The scope of these actions is the more remarkable when one realizes that multiple volunteer networks for an entire county were created from a pool of citizens that numbers in the hundreds rather than

At an Iowa courthouse, three children wait with their father for a foreclosure hearing on the family farm.

the tens of thousands.

Yet, Ross stresses again, "The important thing we did was to set a community of farmers on a search for the truth about what had happened to them. The moment that search began, the community had taken a giant step toward recapturing health—not economic health, for that still eludes us—but emotional health."

Since those early days, the residents of Allerton and the surrounding farms have continued to be an awakened and searching people. In terms of saving farms, not much has been accomplished, but perhaps for the first time a true community has been created.

* * *

If some statements at the beginning of this chapter implied an author's prejudice against the Midwestern farmer, I admit that such a prejudice has been part of my thinking for the last thirty years. It has seemed to me that farmers in this most fertile region of the country have focussed on their own concerns and have exerted a regressive pull on national political and social issues and even on church mission activities. I have wondered if they were willing to share in the necessary hope, work and expense of creating a more just society for the people of the whole country. So now that they are tasting injustice, now that they are facing ruin because of national decisions made for the supposed benefit of the rest of us, part of me wants to say, "I told you so."

But Ross Blount insists that the message is different. "We need always to see difficult experiences as ways of coming to light, of coming to see the commonality of things. We must build on that commonality and make of our experiences opportunities to turn around in our thinking, opportunities to make the link between communities of misfortune. Farmers can understand now what they once could not understand."

Meanwhile, Ross points out, each farm lost is a blow to the overall quality of American life. In little towns out in Iowa, according to him, "for every seven farms lost, one small business closes." In Allerton that translates into just one farm implement dealer operating today where six existed five years ago. It translates into families moving away, school budgets ruined, the further graying of a small piece of the country—a small piece multiplied by thousands of communities. But the minister goes further: "Do *not* believe that it was the inefficient farmer who has been lost," he says. "Rather, it is the progressive farmer who has been hurt, the one who tried to keep up with the latest thinking, the one most willing to take a chance for better crops, better income, better service, including service to the community. I've lost five elders [church officers]—they've gone out of business, fled the town. They were among the most imaginative, creative people we had."

At the time that I am writing, a segment of the farming industry would have us believe that the farm crisis is over, or almost so. Interest rates are down again; some overseas markets have reopened; old-line farmers' organizations—long since captured by the big industrial farm companies—have mitigated their cries of alarm in Washington, D.C.

Good times *are* back—for the *industrial* farm. Owning tens of thousands of acres as well as packing plants and even food marketing chains, the larger operators have renewed access to credit. But what has happened to typical small farmers (small compared to agribusiness operations) has scared off the banks, and even where banks will loan money, the farmers themselves are afraid to incur debt again. And so the failures continue, and for every farm that fails ten farms are sold because their owners, though avoiding failure, find that small-scale operations often don't produce enough income to make the strain worthwhile.

In Iowa, the industrial farming companies have been busy at foreclosure sales, buying up land from discouraged or failed farmers. Ross Blount reports that one of them has acquired 400 failed farms, and employs a crew of more than 100 former owners just to keep the buildings, houses and fences in repair. Canadian farmers, who for decades have concentrated on marketing their crops through cooperative systems, have found it harder in recent years to compete with U.S. companies moving into Canadian farming operations.

From 1986 reports by the U.S. Department of Agriculture and the Congressional Office of Technology Assessment, we know that 300 farms go out of business every day, that by the year 2000 one million U.S. farms will have disappeared, and that industrial farming companies already control 59 million acres of U.S. land. Even before the present spate of farm failures, 75 percent of the 1.3 billion acres of U.S. land owned privately was held by a mere 5 percent of the nation's landowners.

We can be sure that Iowa's or Alberta's fine fields and meadows will continue to produce good crops for the tables of the United States and Canada and a half-dozen other nations: the industrial farms will see to that. But the social dynamics across a continent will have changed. Small-holders will have disappeared; a more feudal landowning class will have arisen, headed by corporation presidents. The marketing system will change; large-scale producers will control pricing with more power than independent or cooperative farmers could ever exert. And the rapport, the sense of peoplehood between folk of the city and folk of the fields that two North American nations once possessed or might have created will fade in the path of farming that regards crop growth in the same light as steel production or banking profits.

Can anything reverse this trend? Ross and Lorena Blount do not know; Joe Brill—now a factory worker in Phoenix—and Blanche do not know; and neither do I. But I do know this: when the last family farmer has left the fields to sit down at the last family farm dinner, when the family farm's tractor has given way to the megamachine of the industrial producer, something of the essence of the American dream will have perished. A basic block will have been pulled from the foundation of our society. We will all be hired hands on that day, and all the sleek young country strummers and singers of Nashville will not be able to recreate a single note of the melody that freedom once played in the fields and barns and houses of the family farm.

CHAPTER 6: A Hard Life in "The Corridor"

> Jesus said, "In a certain city there was a judge who neither feared God nor respected people, and there was a widow in that city who kept coming to the judge and saying, 'Vindicate me against my adversary.' For a while the judge refused, but afterward thought, 'Though I neither fear God nor respect people, yet because this widow bothers me, I will vindicate her, or she will wear me out by her continual coming.'" (Luke 18:2-5)

Jesus talks about a persistent widow to illustrate the relationship between prayer and the longing for God's justice. In one way, the story offers an example of human limitations: if even an unrighteous judge will finally act on behalf of a woman who has been wronged, then how much more will God, who is righteousness itself, do for those who cry to God for justice day and night (see verses 6-8). In another way, the story presents a positive illustration of the power of complaining about what is wrong. The complainer in this case is one of the most vulnerable members of society: a widow is a woman without a male protector in a society where men controlled economic, religious and legal rights. Although women today have gained much more freedom in these spheres, women without the protection of men or money still form one of society's most vulnerable groups. And the responsibility for raising children by oneself increases that vulnerability, whether a woman is divorced, unmarried or—now in fewer instances— widowed.

As Jesus portrays it, complaining is not whining or self-pity but an act of strength. From the knowledge that weakness has been exploited springs the sense of justice, with its elements of grief and anger. The Bible is full of such complaints—in the biblical view, complaints clearly do not detract from praise of God (in fact, even God complains sometimes!). Prophets often voice the people's complaints to God as well as God's complaints to the people.

The duty of a good ruler, as the Bible defines it, is to administer God's justice: "May the ruler defend the cause of the poor of the people, give deliverance to the needy, and crush the oppressor!"

(Psalm 72:4). When the ruler, or government, fails to fulfill this duty, then consistent complaining by the poor or their advocates is in order. The widow in the parable was left to protest by herself, without an advocate—and proved herself competent to do so.

"The poor" in North America today are in large part composed of women—and the children they are raising. The name given to this growing phenomenon is "the feminization of poverty." Its causes are manifold: lack of jobs that pay enough to raise a family, lack of education and training for better jobs, lack of good child-care facilities, failure to receive court-ordered child support from absent fathers, lack of back-up social services for poor women who work for wages. Popular opinion to the contrary, women do not get rich on welfare. In no state in the U.S. does the combination of Aid to Families with Dependent Children (AFDC) and food stamps—which constitute welfare—provide income above the poverty level. In the U.S., the average welfare payment for each person is $3.97 per day; food stamps supply about 50 cents per meal per person.

The AFDC system, which was designed in the 1930s to allow single mothers to stay at home with children, is self-defeating. Payments have not kept up with inflation. When a woman starts to work outside the home, AFDC payments are cut and medical benefits are lost, sometimes for the children as well as for the mother. Credit allowed for child-care expenses is below the cost of adequate child care. A woman who earns a minimum wage in a job with no benefits may decide that it would be better for her children if she stopped working and tried to cope on welfare. For black and Hispanic women, who are likely to earn lower incomes and have less access to decent housing than white mothers, this dilemma must be faced frequently.

Sweden, France and several other Western nations have assistance systems that are more supportive of working women—and in any country a mother's earnings now provide the best guarantee of sufficient family income. As we are about to see, a job training program for a single mother in Canada provides more supplementary support for a longer time than is the case in the U.S. But the path to self-sufficiency is plagued with pitfalls in both countries. Among the worst of these are the stigma of receiving "welfare" or "relief" in societies that assume that anyone who works hard enough can make it, and the intrusion into one's private life that occurs as a matter of course when a social service bureaucracy controls the household finances.

*   *   *

Anyone who has had experience with the welfare system knows the complaints of the vulnerable. I will call the people who expressed them to me Jean Hughes,[*] and her son, Daniel. Jean is forty-two years old, Daniel is nineteen, and they live in a two-bedroom apartment in Toronto's Jane-Finch Corridor, an area, notorious for its drug traffic, around the intersection of the city's main thoroughfares, Jane Street and Finch Avenue.

Jean was brought to Canada from England at age eight with her younger brother and older sister by her mother, who was recently divorced and wanted a "new start." The family lived together in the town of Kitchener, Ontario. The girl was precocious, both physically and mentally. But distaste for study, and the teasing of schoolboys about her early-blossoming figure, caused her to leave school when she reached the eighth grade. She never went back.

Jean Hughes married at twenty-two. In retrospect, the union seems to have been modelled on that of her parents. Within a year she appeared in court to obtain a divorce on the grounds of abuse and adultery. The man who had been her husband disappeared—no support payments for Jean and young Daniel from him—and the young immigrant was alone in Canada with the responsibility for raising a child. She thus joined the masses of women—3.5 million in the U.S., 500,000 in Canada—who raise their children on incomes below the poverty level.

Without skills, without education, without family, Jean's situation was desperate. She could not go out to work while Daniel was an infant. Later, given the area where she lived, she did not feel comfortable about available baby-sitters, even if she could have afforded to hire one on the kind of wages she might have earned. For Jean, no options were open but life on a "Mothers' Allowance," the name Canada gives to the form of public assistance that is called "Aid to Families with Dependent Children" in the United States.

When Jean Hughes applied for and received her first Mothers' Allowance check, she didn't know what was involved. The money—now $500 Canadian each month, but much less nineteen years ago—did indeed keep the wolf from the door, though rent

---

[*] Not their real surnames.

consumed a quarter of it, even in Jane-Finch Corridor. There were additional allowances for such necessities as the child's dental care (some of her own dental care was covered, too, but not all). But by the time telephone and transportation expenses had been paid, Jean found herself "lucky at the end of the month to have a cent left to buy a pair of pantyhose."

Existence on Mothers' Allowance had disadvantages beyond the system's meager economics. Along with the allowance came a social worker. Despite the suggestion of help implied by the title, a social worker for a public assistance agency is one who is entitled to concern herself or himself with every facet of an assisted mother's life. Jean found her social workers variously pleasant and unpleasant, competent and incompetent (the personnel assigned to her case changed frequently). Some of them even became her friends. But she never overcame her resentment of the social workers' legal "right" to concern themselves with her affairs.

In addition, Jean found that recipients of Mothers' Allowance in Canada suffer from much public prejudice. Common mythology perceives them as dirty, shiftless, unable to discipline their children. Jean, who has the compulsive busyness and the lace-doily tidiness of the English lower middle class, was particularly offended when such faults were ascribed to her because of her financial situation. To her, a social worker's probably unintentional sweep of a hand over a chair cushion before sitting down became a mortal blow to self-esteem. "She obviously thought my house wasn't clean," Jean recalls.

Daniel's school experience was similarly marred, Jean believes, by his teachers' knowledge that he was the child of someone on public assistance. "The boy has no great head for abstract learning," she says, "and always has had to work hard for what he gets in school. But he is good with his hands and quick to understand the idea of a machine. Any machine. Somebody, I should think, could have taken an interest in him." But nobody did, except for one worker—a school behavioral consultant whom Jean has revered ever since. Daniel, now almost twenty, will graduate from high school this year after a difficult school career.

For fifteen years Jean stayed home, receiving her assistance check each month. Those years constituted one long erosion of her self-esteem. "It got so that I was afraid to meet people, or even to go out and about." A thousand times she considered, and rejected, the idea of getting a job: "I had no skills at all, and that meant the only job I could have had was waitressing. But waitressing means weekend work—and here I was with a young son, and living in one of the city's worst neighborhoods. Why, right down on the corner outside my home they sell all kinds of drugs, and the police do nothing. I just could not abandon my son to that kind of environment."

Nevertheless, there came a day when concern for her own mental health obliged Jean to trust Danny's advancing maturity and take a chance. She read in the newspaper about a cleaning service, "Merrie Maids." This company sends women out daily to do housework for a fee, on the same basis by which some employment agencies supply temporary office workers.

Jean, vigorous and strong, seemed a "natural" to the Merrie Maid people, and they hired her. Today, four years later, the company supplies her with a car (she must buy the gasoline herself) and has given her a "territory," the Willowdale area of the city. In relative terms, Jean's business has prospered, and she enjoys the variety of social contacts that go with the job. As for Danny— well, he has survived.

Jean Hughes's employment is linked to a "Job Incentive Program" designed to gradually move people off Mothers' Allowance and into the job market. Under the incentive program, an employed mother continues to receive the difference between her earnings and the monthly Mothers' Allowance set by the government. Jean is proud that recently her job earnings for two consecutive months were high enough to reduce the Allowance amount to just $2.50. Soon, she hopes, the government will have to pay nothing.

Jean has been working with Merrie Maids long enough now to feel good about herself and about the program. But, as so often happens with job training and "workfare" programs in both Canada and the U.S., the Incentive Program is hedged round with so many limitations that much of the pleasure is erased. In Jean's case the problem was a government mistake. Although her employer sent Mothers' Allowance the required monthly reports of Jean's earnings, six months elapsed before the program caught up with this new data. During that period Jean received almost $4,000 in allowances that she was not entitled to. Says Jean, "I didn't understand the program entirely. It's true that I knew I would be cut back in allowance sometime. But I thought the time in which the full check continued was some sort of grace period in which, perhaps, I could get caught up on back bills. . . ."

But such was not the case. Today Jean is faced with repeated, strongly worded demands for repayment of the sum. She has no way to meet the obligation. "They are even threatening to collect it from my old-age benefit, when I get that old," she says.

Next year, when Daniel graduates, Jean's currently subsidized rent for a mean apartment on a mean Toronto street will double. It is by no means sure that Daniel, with only a high-school diploma, will readily find employment that will allow him to help out at home. Meanwhile, the government continues its efforts to collect Jean's "overdrawn" $4,000. And the harried woman gets up each morning at five-thirty, leaves the house at six-thirty so she can get to her first customer, labors through the day in a succession of homes, and returns to her apartment after five each evening. She then must call each customer for the next day to confirm her appointments. It isn't much of a life.

But Jean Hughes isn't downhearted. Instead, she is upbeat. "I could never go back to total reliance on Mothers' Allowance," she declares. "Not now, when I've had a taste of semi-independence." Still, she remains close enough to those fifteen years of total dependence on assistance to have some definite opinions on how such programs are administered. Says Jean:

> I wish that somebody, somewhere, would get across to governments and to people in general the idea that most women want very much to be off Mothers' Allowance. It's just that the government makes it so difficult, so hard, to put the transition together. Most women on Mothers' Allowance are not lazy; what they lack is encouragement. Does it have to be that supervisory agencies are so cold, so rule-bound? Couldn't they devise a way to be a little human, a little patient, and a little helpful in ways that are emotionally supportive? Believe me, it is not *being* poor that almost destroys you; it is the way that people *treat* you when you are poor. Even those who are supposed to do the helping. . . .

CHAPTER 7: Falling through the Net

"In the thought of one who is at ease there is contempt for
misfortune; it is ready for those whose feet slip."
   (Job 12:5).

"You who live in the clefts of the rock,
      who hold the height of the hill,
Though you make your nest as high as the eagle's,
      I will bring you down from there,"
      says the Lord.
   (Jeremiah 49:16b)

"Woe to you that are full now, for you shall hunger. . ."
   (Luke 6: 25a)

From Genesis to Revelation, the Scriptures abound in stories
and predictions that underscore the transitory nature of
prosperity and the possibility that ruin—economic, social or
moral—can befall any or all of us at any time. In light of these
stories, biblical faith can be understood as trust in the eternal
reality of God's good purpose in a world which, from our human
point of view, can seem full of misfortune.

Most of us, it is true, don't spend a lot of time pondering the
moral nature of the universe—thinking about whether it is the
goodness of God's purpose or the badness of ruin and misfortune
that determine the way things are. We just go on living our daily
lives as though we intended to live forever in our present estate
or a better one. But when, spurred by some dire event in our
own or others' lives, we do turn to the question of why, if the
world is created by a loving God, human beings can suffer so
much from reversals of fortune, we find a biblical resource written
to order.

The story of Job is one of the most curious tales to have survived
in the Old Testament canon. A "blameless and upright" believer
struggles to understand the reasons for the overwhelming
deprivations visited upon him. In Job's case, the drama is intensified by picturing Satan as an examiner who has been given license
to test Job in every way short of taking his life. Although most
Christians do not view their own troubles as prompted by a

malicious, superhuman figure, and although most of our trials are not as severe as Job's—whose cattle are stolen, children killed, and body ulcerated—we can identify with the questions he hurls at the universe and its God (see Job 1:6-2:9).

When Job's life lies in ruins, three friends—Eliphaz the Temanite, Bildad the Shuhite and Zophar the Naamathite—come to call on him. They begin a long dialogue with Job about the origin of his troubles, a dialogue that continues until the latter pages of the book, when the Lord God appears and enters the discussion. Though brokenhearted and desperate, Job will not allow himself to rail against the Almighty for his misfortunes. But the three friends don't make endurance any easier. For openers, Eliphaz upbraids Job for being downcast: "Is not your fear of God your confidence?" (4:6a). Eliphaz then urges Job to call on God for help, implying subtly that Job must have done something wrong, perhaps even been *too* righteous, since "happy is the one whom God reproves," who should not despise "the chastening of the Almighty" (5:17).

Bildad is scarcely more helpful. He accuses Job of a false, blustering courage (8:2), tells him to study history in order to understand his plight (8:8), and bids him be patient because better days are coming (8:21). Then Zophar urges Job to take a real, down-to-earth view of his difficulties, remembering that God always sees human evil (11:11). If Job will just own up to his faults, Zophar insists, then God will surely let him forget his misery, recalling it only "as waters that have passed away" (11:16).

The three friends are prosperous individuals, still secure in the abundance of material and familial comforts that Job himself had once enjoyed. They are his peers, we must understand, who—though doubtless in kindness and concern—now presume to prescribe for him. The remedies they propose for his difficulties are based on certain assumptions about the causes of those difficulties. Such remedies are, of course, the hardest kind of advice to accept, and Job accepts it no more graciously than would the rest of us. "I have understanding as well as you," he reminds his friends; "I am not inferior to you." Therefore (I paraphrase), will you please quit uttering these platitudes! (12:3).

* * *

I thought often of Job and his friends in 1985 and '86 when I lost my employment and went broke. I put my own story here among the accounts of others who have suffered, and still suffer, much worse disasters than I, because of what the experience showed me about the primitive methods of helping people in trouble that are practiced in most churches.

Here are the bare bones of the story:

- In 1983, when I was fifty-six, my employer closed the publication where I worked for twenty-six years; my job was gone.
- I sought a job diligently, using all my "networks," but received not one nibble in four months. So, determined to work at *something*, I staked everything on a publication of my own. In the end, the capital available to me was not sufficient for a venture of this kind. Circulation kept growing, but the publication failed within two years.
- Thereafter, we were forced to sell our house to satisfy federal business tax liabilities, because my own resources plus considerable sums from family and friends had been exhausted in last-minute attempts to keep the venture going.
- At last came the day when there was nothing to do but close the company bank account (empty anyway), lock the office and notify creditors that nothing was left of the business. By that time, there was nothing left for the family either.

A number of surprises were now in store for this idle breadwinner. First came the discovery that the route from small business proprietor to public assistance roll was likely to be very direct. No matter how much they have paid into government unemployment compensation funds on behalf of others, proprietors of businesses in the U.S. and Canada have no access to such benefits themselves. This still seems unfair to me, especially when the businesses involved are very small.

A second surprise involved the mechanics of going broke. We had the services of a good lawyer who was also a family friend. We wished to avoid bankruptcy proceedings, partly from distaste (it's not part of our cultural tradition), partly because we intended to try to repay our creditors, and partly because we did not want to involve another friend who had kindly agreed to serve as vice president of the corporation. No problem, said the lawyer: bankruptcy provides for an equitable distribution of assets—and your firm has no assets to distribute. He informed our creditors of the firm's collapse and cautioned us to make no contact with them lest it appear that we were assuming personal liability. I waited for a storm to break.

And nothing happened—nothing! It is not only creditors who feel that some horrendous fate should await heads of businesses who cannot pay their debts; I felt so, too. As weeks and months went by, I told myself again and again that it ought not to be so easy to walk away from the debts of a business you have started—though proprietors of small businesses certainly find exalted models for doing so among some who manage large corporations. I even called myself foolish for my attitude; after all, you can't get milk from a dead cow. Nevertheless, the relative ease with which creditors' claims are handled became for me a part of the heavy burden that everyone without employment carries: a burden of self-imposed (and sometimes publicly imposed) guilt.

Extra weight soon accrued to the burden. My wife and I had always said—quite self-righteously as it turns out—that we were not "materialists." We considered such items as a decent car or comfortable home very pleasant, thank you, but not among life's sine qua nons. So, busy with lawyers, accountants, and my own emotions, I didn't notice how much my valorous wife, Sue, had begun to withdraw into herself. She ate little, spoke little. She was grieving silently for that sunlit house, for every tree the two of us had planted in its yard, that we must now leave. One day she collapsed and had to be hospitalized. We had no medical insurance, not a bleeding cent.[*]

In our country, hospitals are, if not profit-making, then at least balance-the-books institutions. If you lag behind in paying a bill, we learned, they will report you to the credit bureau far sooner than other businesses will. Some of them won't even admit you unless they feel certain they will get paid.

I don't say that I lied. I did give an optimistic estimate of the speed with which I could pay the bill. But I *would* have lied myself green in the face to get treatment for my wife. Seven days later and $4,000 deeper in debt, she was back with me again, worn out but composed. The hospital and its doctors had done much to heal her. But the adverse credit report on our "slow pay" made our recovery that much more difficult—and added to the guilt.

About this time Henry came to our house. Henry was from

---

[*] In Canada, most people are covered by health insurance plans administered by the provinces. For some, coverage is an employee benefit, but all citizens and landed immigrants are eligible for health insurance; for people unable to afford the premium, a government subsidy will cover up to three-quarters of the cost. See the Appendix.

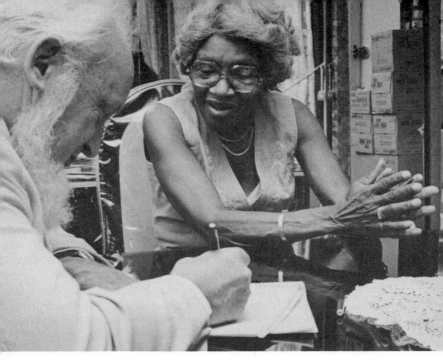

Journalist Jim Gittings talks with Clara M. Hale, whose care for children of drug addicted mothers led to the founding of Hale House in Harlem. Some children now at Hale House (below) were born with AIDS.

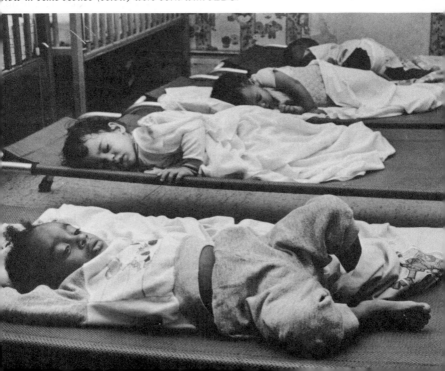

the deacon's committee at church, and he brought a sack of
groceries plus about three days' worth of meals cooked and frozen
by his wife. Now if you are going to send someone to assist a
once reasonably affluent person down on his or her luck, send
somebody like Henry. He began by joking that I had been awarded
the "Turkey of the Month" citation. And down in the bottom of
that sack of groceries he had hidden a bottle of very good Scotch
whiskey (I'm sure that was Henry's own contribution, and not
from the deacons' fund). Otherwise, there was flour and cereal,
some meat, a package of cheese, and so on.

Henry is younger than I. On occasion, he had been in church
school classes that I taught. No scholar (except in his line), Henry
shared few of my interests and almost none of my political views.
What he was, and is, is a solid businessman, one of that army
of entrepreneurs of which the U.S., thank God, has millions. But
the point is that I found it harder than almost anything in my
life to accept that gift of groceries from Henry. And if it was hard
for me, it was twice as hard for Sue.

Henry came back twice before we were through. But he would
have returned a dozen times if necessary, I know, and the church
to which we belonged would have come up a dozen times with
the money to fill his sack. Later I will comment about methods,
but for the moment, please hear this clearly: these were and are
people of good hearts and open hands.

Eventually we had to depend on the church, through the
minister's discretionary fund, for several hundred dollars as well.
By that time, I felt so devoid of honor or worth that asking was
almost easy. Again, the pastor gave graciously; no promise of
repayment was exacted.

The truth is that in the long course of the crisis we did not
think very clearly. I continued to grind out free-lance articles for
low-paying journals; such work did not provide a fifth of what
we needed. But the income did feed my hope—and my foolish
determination to stay away from the welfare office as well. Given
Pennsylvania's policies toward unemployed males, I probably
would not have qualified for assistance. But Sue would have; she
would have gotten *something*.

Meantime, my brothers and sisters did what they could, given
distance, family needs, children in college. Friends in New York
and elsewhere, as well as in our own town, assisted us. The total
of this help was not enough to live on. No work turned up, and
I couldn't afford the travel necessary to search for something in

my line. As for a job in the town where we lived—well, its unemployment rate was 18 percent, and nothing was open to people my age.

Eventually, after a year of next-to-no earned income, two things happened. First, a church-related study center near New York City offered us the use of a house while I searched for a job (we stayed eleven months); second, I was given part-time research work by one of my denomination's national committees. With basic necessities—a roof, a little money—nailed down, I set out with greater energy and composure on my job hunt. A few months later an old friend steered me toward a writing job with an established charitable agency. Now I am fully employed again, and we have begun to make some strides toward eventual economic recovery. That recovery will never be complete: in six years I will reach the customary retirement age of sixty-five (though I hope to work longer), and we are only beginning our efforts to make amends to those who suffered losses through my business venture.

* * *

At this point in my story and in this book, my feelings and conclusions from this experience have come to bear so heavily on my thoughts about both being poor and helping the poor that I want to state them openly.

- After having my job terminated by my employer of twenty-six years, and after hearing and reading about hundreds of thousands of other Americans similarly tossed out of jobs after long service, I never want to hear an employer mention employee loyalty again.
- Most doctors I know are nice people. Do they know that the practice some of them follow in contracting with private debt collection services puts them, like loan companies, among the agencies that are the first to add suffering to people who have been wiped out economically? In my case, I can assure the good doctors that their collection services did not speed the payment of any bills by one hour.
- Most counties have a medical assistance program for people in economic trouble. It is to these programs that hospitals steer potential patients when they have no medical insurance. I still remember the kindly lady who tried (very politely) to get me to come in and fill out the proper forms during a period of emotional crisis, thus forcing me to leave my

wife's side. This exemplifies the many ways that bureaucratic systems keep humane people busy trying to get those who are poor to conform to inhuman processes.

• Most important: A church deacons' committee is a good service medium and worth working to improve. My suggestions:

1. Set enough "ears" to work in the congregation to ensure that the committee learns of employment or family crises early in their development. (I am referring to financial crises in particular, but these steps may be useful in other kinds of trouble as well.)

2. Move quickly to make contact with the troubled person or family—through a friend, if necessary—to determine precise needs. Do not arrive with a food basket when the phone bill is the immediate concern.

3. Once contact is made, try to get the *whole* story: what are immediate needs, what will be needed next, is there health insurance, etc.

4. Get a man to relate to the males in the family, a woman to the females. *Stay in touch.*

5. When you can, proceed on a problem-solving rather than an emergency-meeting basis.

6. Don't expect the family at church for a while, but don't let them lose touch with the church just because they are absent.

7. Ask some people who are employed or knowledgeable in an unemployed person's field to help him or her organize a job hunt.

When I reflect about my experience on the edge of economic destruction, two aspects are unforgettable. First, I did not want to be a word-breaker, and economic downs and ups make word-breakers of honest men and women. Second, every day that I was unemployed I remembered how hard my father had worked to win a fingerhold in the lower middle class, to get an education for his children and to provide security for his family. I felt like the traitor in the family tree, the one who was falling through the branches and would hit the ground.

But what my father had worked so hard to achieve became precisely the saving element in my situation: we *were* middle-class people; we had relationships; there were people to whom we could turn and skills we had to market. Not everybody is so fortunate.

I had something else that not everyone possesses: my continuing belief that neither God nor the universe is malevolent. It is true that some part of me felt, whether the feeling came from faith or some other source, that I was guilty of something or I wouldn't have been in trouble. The feeling nagged at me, made me blue, took the edge of buoyancy from the energies I brought to each day.

Yet, reflecting on those days a year later, I have the distinct impression that the guilt I felt was not the pathological kind. It seemed as sure as sunrise to me that sooner or later matters would take a turn for the better. I was sure of that eventual turn for three reasons. First, I had faith in the communities with which I had identified myself—not faith in my town, but in my friends in the town; not faith in the church, but in my friends in the church. Someone from one of these communities would help me find something to do, I was sure. Second, I believed—the proper phrase really is "had faith"—that years of constructive service to church, community and nation (in descending order of priority) must outweigh the blunders or improprieties of my latest publishing venture. At work in my mind was, I suppose, a confidence in justice. Finally, I had confidence that God had a further use for me, somewhere, and would not permit any human agency to frustrate those purposes.

I am aware that people who choose not to believe will snort at the three elements of my comfort. I am aware, too, that people who believe in a God who goes about punishing and rewarding people to prepare them for a day of judgment on which believers will be rescued and their neighbors damned will find my thought processes during this period ridiculously optimistic. But to those who cling fast to the idea that God is developing the kingdom of love and peace and justice in this world, and that God's kingdom is one in which each of us may rightfully claim a place—well, such persons will understand at once how such a believer is protected from debilitating guilt and is freed to step through any door to another room, another day.

Those who work toward and expect God's kingdom are indeed a curious group. When our worlds explode around us, we rise up from the debris to set out again on our search for signs of order and grace in a shattered universe.

CHAPTER 8: A Criminal Dimension

> There were some present at that very time who told him
> of the Galileans whose blood Pilate had mingled with their
> sacrifices. And he answered them, "Do you think that these
> Galileans were worse sinners than all the other Galileans,
> because they suffered thus? I tell you, No; but unless you
> repent you will all likewise perish. Or those eighteen upon
> whom the tower in Siloam fell and killed them, do you
> think that they were worse offenders than all the others
> who dwelt in Jerusalem? I tell you, No; but unless you
> repent you will all likewise perish." (Luke 13:1-5)

Many Jews in Jesus' time, like many Christians today, thought
that painful experiences were evidence of God's displeasure.
Nowhere is this belief more of a trap than in the attitudes of
prosperous folk toward those who are dogged by misfortune. We
have a habit of linking prosperity to merit, especially when we
are the prosperous. Carrying the same attitude a step further, we
sometimes feel that misfortune stems from indolence or vice, as
we noted in the preceding chapter.

In the verses from Luke quoted above, Jesus comments on two
events of interest from the news of his day. One was an early
example of state encroachment on the sacred precincts of the Jewish
temple. Roman soldiers had killed some country folk who had
run afoul of the law while in town to offer religious sacrifices.
The other was an industrial accident like those we read about
in newspapers almost every day; eighteen people were killed in
the collapse of a building under construction.

No doubt Jesus' listeners, learning of these events, pondered
the random nature of tragedy as we do, asking "Why them?" just
as we ask "Why me?" when we lose our job or the house burns
down or a beloved child dies. But when Jesus was asked, "Were
those who died the worst offenders?" he answered with a flat
"No." Interestingly, Jesus did not disassociate himself from the
idea that *some* things that happen to us are a recompense for
misdeeds. He was, after all, rooted in the tradition of his people,
and the Hebrew Scriptures were and are ambivalent on this point.
We read about Uriah, an innocent person slain for reasons for

which he had no responsibility (II Samuel 11:1-17). But we also learn of cases like that of King Nebuchadnezzar, who became mad from the sin of pride (Daniel 4:19-37), and of Job, an apparently blameless person visited by a series of troubles as a kind of test (Job 1:6-12). Jesus did not say that punishment by trouble never occurs.

What Jesus did say on this most interesting occasion was that his listeners should not *focus* on the moral inadequacies of others as a possible source of their misfortunes. Instead, they should consider their own condition: "Unless you repent, you will all likewise perish." This abrupt reversal, in which a question is held up to the asker like a mirror, was a practice Jesus used again and again in his teaching. We are told in Luke 16, for example, about a poor man covered with sores who was sitting at a rich man's gate. Suddenly it is the rich man suffering in hell to whom our gaze is directed (Luke 16:19-31). Or again, Jesus mentions a person who has been beaten. Our interest quickens: a crime story is about to unfold. But with a flick of the narrator's wrist, we must suddenly consider the ethics of certain eminent travellers, and then weigh ourselves as neighbors (Luke 10:30-37).

Jesus' insistence that we turn our curiosity from our neighbors' afflictions to an examination of our own responsibility follows a time-honored teaching method in the Jewish tradition. In the Introduction we heard Moses urge open-handedness toward the poor, not in expectation of repayment but so that one's own undertakings might prosper and because "you were a slave in Egypt and the Lord your God redeemed you" (Deuteronomy 15:15). For Moses, both self-interest and the memory of one's own origins dictate that one become a partisan for the poor. Yet Moses is willing to be a passionate advocate for this people even when they do not keep their commitments. Once he quarreled with God on behalf of his suffering, rebellious flock (Exodus 32:31-32). "Blot me out of thy book," he said to God, "if thou wilt not forgive this people." We are reminded of Abraham pleading with God to spare the people of the cities of the plain (Genesis 18:17-25), and of God's rebuke to Jonah for that strongminded prophet's failure to adopt a similar attitude—"Should I not pity Nineveh, that great city" (Jonah 4:1-11).

We Christians are a tough-minded bunch: we are not so easily put off, even by our Savior's words, from the notion that some people get their "just deserts" in life. To say to us, as Jesus did, "Judge not lest ye be judged" (Matthew 7:1-2), may silence our tongues but not our thoughts. Some people, we insist, *deserve* what they get—and some *should* get what they deserve.

As a society we have devised official ways to ensure that some people do get a measure of what they deserve for their misdeeds. In planning this book, I checked some U.S. demographic statistics. To my astonishment, more than 750,000 persons were listed as "incarcerated." Jurists assure us that the figure will exceed one million well before the century is out. Most of these imprisoned people are young men of black, Hispanic and white working-class origins (though the number of women is increasing). In Canada also, most prisoners are men, a large proportion of them young men. And in both nations, almost all of these are poor.

That poor people get into trouble with the law should not surprise us. Sometimes, minor crimes derive directly from their financial position: for example, false swearing on a loan application—not hard to do when the children are hungry—or resisting eviction, even with physical force. We also know that desperation breeds violence and that some individuals become practitioners of violence. To visit a prison cell in the United States is to see—in over 50 percent of cases, in some states—a young black man, one of the (at least) 45 percent of black youths who are unemployed. These and a cohort of white youths of similar ages are, often, extremely violent people. The rate of violent crime is rising in Canada, especially in western provinces.[*] When we read that one or another of these wreakers of violence has been convicted of robbery, assault or murder, we are likely to hope that he (or she) will get the long sentence the crime deserves. Victims' families and community leaders plead with parole boards to refuse early release for such criminals.

To be a partisan for the poor does not mean to deny an element of "just deserts" in the conviction and imprisonment of violent persons (although most poor people are neither criminal nor violent). Nor does it mean to absolve such persons of responsibility by shifting their guilt to a vague entity called "society." But in looking for a way to take seriously Jesus' emphasis on our own repentance, I resolved to get to know a criminal in an area where I had lived and to hear that person's story in order to see whether decisions or actions taken by myself and other citizens were in

---

[*] Although in Canada the number of adult prison inmates for every 100,000 people in the population is less than half that of the U.S. (97 inmates in Canada to 207 in the U.S. per 100,000 population, in recent years).

any way reflected in the person's development and crimes.

* * *

As I sought to keep my resolution, I quickly found ample evidence to confirm a hunch: that the society of prisoners belongs in a book about poverty in North America. The person I found came from a household crippled by low income (among a number of other causes) and had grown up in other low-income households. As an adult she consorted with people of uncertain incomes. Yet, incredibly, vast sums of money have been spent on her or in her name, and some of that money was used to *keep* her poor. Her name is Mary Ellen Flannery.*

Mary Ellen was born to alcoholic parents, her mother a waitress and occasional prostitute, her father a petty thief. As a small child, well under five, she wandered the streets of her eastern Pennsylvania neighborhood, irregularly fed and washed. The only source of affection in her young life was a grandmother who dropped in from time to time to try to get Mary Ellen's mother to straighten up. At age five and a half, the child played lookout outside an apartment house while her parents robbed it. When she was six, her father decamped for Miami and a recurring residence in prisons of the Sunshine State. Half a year later another "father" moved in; this one sexually fondled the little girl.

Not surprisingly, Mary Ellen became a "court child" before she was seven. To say that she lost something important when her new status was thrust upon her is not to discredit the child-care professionals who thereafter supervised her "case." They carried caseloads of up to sixty children each. As a "case," Mary Ellen required something called a "disposition." The purpose of a disposition was not principally, as one might suppose, to create or protect a healthy child, but to bring a child without too much fuss through a chain of foster homes to an age when—taxpayers, rejoice!—she or he would pass from the care of county and state and on to adulthood.

A child's path from a sexually aberrational household to a foster home passes through a "shelter" for children under diagnostic study. There, professionally dispassionate women and men interview you, test you, evaluate you, in a process that lasts for days or weeks. Except for the matrons, the staff goes home at five o'clock. Their departure leaves you in the company of other

---

* Not her real name. No real names of people are used in this chapter.

six-to-twelve-year-olds from all sorts of backgrounds. Mary Ellen learned that there are "funny games" in the shelter too and lots of new words. If you are little, you can also get beaten up in shelters and are generally at the mercy of the bigger children.

Mary Ellen celebrated her seventh birthday in the home of a Mr. and Mrs. Jones. She remembers them as "nice people," though Mr. Jones "got mad, sometimes." The Joneses soon learned what the social worker had not told them—that they were taking in a wild creature, a child who did not know and could not give affection. The little girl's rages, her atrocious and irregular eating habits, her language, her wakefulness caused more commotion than the money paid for her keep was worth. Back she went to the shelter, for the first of seven returns before the age of ten.

In her second foster home, Mary Ellen was again sexually abused. She does not say much about her feelings, but the results were that she would never again look at an adult as the objective, reliable "other" that most children see; from her experiences, an adult male became a person who wants sexual gratification from you even when you are seven, and thus someone you must be wary of. She ran away, sleeping in the streets for two nights before being picked up and returned to the shelter.

Home Three kept Mary Ellen nearly a year before moving to Florida. Home Four had three children already and deemed her a "corrupting influence." Home Five was in a black neighborhood, Mary Ellen was one of only three white girls in her grade, so she ran away. In Home Six, her foster father had a heart attack and had to cut down on his responsibilities.

Mary Ellen never stayed in a school long enough to belong, so she formed her friendships among other marginal children like herself. Each year she became angrier, tougher, more resentful of authority in any form, more certain that every person has a price and no person, especially a male, a principle.

Oddly, she progressed from grade to grade in school during these years. Her promotions resulted in part from a then-current educational belief that schools should not damage children's self-esteem by holding them back. But this disturbed child was bright, too, and learned quickly, even in the educational shambles that passed for a shelter school. She read widely: paperbacks in the shelter dayrooms, the Bible, the Book of Mormon, whatever came her way.

Religion brushed against Mary Ellen's life at a number of points. By arrangement, her mother came a few times during her sober periods to take the child to the Roman Catholic church of her family's tradition. Her grandmother also came once or twice a year by bus to pick her up at the latest foster home and give her a day at church and Sunday dinner. Then the grandmother died, and Mary Ellen's last natural source of affection perished with her. Foster father Number Six belonged to a pentecostal congregation—one of the few associated with the United Church of Christ—to which he regularly took Mary Ellen. Mostly the girl liked church, though she never made any friends there. But she cannot remember any pastor whose concern about her survived a change of foster family.

Mary Ellen and her mother both recall a strange interval when she briefly returned to her mother's household. The mother had apparently won a skirmish in her battle with alcohol. Mary Ellen remembers cooked meals, shopping trips, and a movie enjoyed together. But in attempting to recreate a relationship, the mother began to confide her own youthful misadventures to Mary Ellen. This contributed to Mary Ellen's sense of herself as a "bad seed" whose unpleasant experiences were foreordained by the character and fate of her parents. Before long, the experiment blew up; the mother returned to her alcohol and Mary Ellen to the streets. At nine, she was back in the shelter, waiting for her next "disposition."

Then began a series of partly tragic events that have proved in the long run creative. Mary Ellen was placed in the home of Perry and Martha Blaine, who were prepared to love her. A childless couple in their early thirties, the Blaines were newcomers to the middle class, he a laborer's son who had become an accountant, she a teacher with similar origins. Paid $110 a month to care for Mary Ellen, the couple took their responsibility seriously enough for Martha to quit her job to care for the youngster. During Mary Ellen's first summer with the Blaines, they took her to England for a never-to-be-forgotten vacation. The Blaines insisted on church attendance, so for more than a year Mary Ellen took part in activities at a local Presbyterian church.

Martha Blaine has thought long about a foster child's relationship to the community around her. She remembers, for example, taking Mary Ellen to a department store one fall to buy school clothes:

> I did not buy clothing of particularly high quality; just the sort of thing I would have bought her if she had been my own child—a little jacket, shoes, a dress, a skirt and blouse. We had been told not to worry about clothing, just to buy

what was necessary and send in the bills. But the agency sent the receipts back marked "disallowed." When I protested, I was told I had spent too much. When this happened a second time, we got the message: we were not to dress Mary Ellen like an ordinary child of our school district; we were to dress her like a court child.

The Blaines had also been told not to worry about the cost of medical care for Mary Ellen. "Just give this to the doctor of your choice," said the caseworker, handing them a card issued by a state agency. But when Martha took Mary Ellen to their family doctor, he was kind but refused to handle billing through the state. So did another doctor; finally one agreed to take responsibility for her medical care.

As a teacher, Martha found school officials' lack of interest particularly galling:

It isn't that I didn't understand the roots of their attitude: a court child is in and out, starts terms late as often as not, is required to be absent for home visitations, evaluations, trips here and there. Sure it must be discouraging for a teacher! What's more, almost every court child is in emotional trouble. I should have thought that a professional response would have been to "pour it on," take extra pains, reach out further. But it wasn't. The response was to ignore the child. And that's what happens, the caseworker told me, in nine cases out of ten.

While the Blaines fought outsiders on behalf of Mary Ellen, battles with the girl herself arose at home. She had never adjusted to regular hours of sleep or play, nor did she prove able to endure regular school attendance—she was often tardy or "sick" and increasingly truant. Attempting to assert authority, Perry Blaine found himself alternately facing a trembling child who feared abuse and a screaming wildcat prepared to hurl dishes at his head. Martha, trying her hand, found herself either cursed roundly or treated with freezing, sullen anger.

Several times Mary Ellen ran away. Each time, brought back by police, she waited to hear the Blaines telephone her caseworker to have her sent back to the shelter. But they never obliged her. Instead, they tried, and tried again, to win her love.

The Blaines, of course, are not perfect. Martha Blaine is a quick-tempered woman whose sense of humor can be as sharp as her anger. Perry Blaine, though endlessly patient and kindly in manner, can seem paralyzed in moments of crisis. Yet it is hard to fault the couple's dealings with Mary Ellen. The angry child, now turning twelve, escalated her challenges to their affection, as if determined to provoke rejection.

Remembering her days at the Blaines, Mary Ellen says now: "It almost paid off. I did really love them; nobody else had ever cared that much about me. But I got to be twelve, and [gesturing toward her breasts] I was big already, and I got on drugs."

Perry and Martha never learned just how that happened; all they knew was that they came home one evening to find their house ransacked, all portable valuables taken and Mary Ellen gone—this time for good.

She did not go far. On the outskirts of Philadelphia are six or seven little industrial cities, each with a drug culture in orbit around the larger metropolitan subculture. In one or another of these Mary Ellen could have been found at any time during the next four years if any person or agency had looked very hard. She "hung out" with other young people (and some not so young) who centered their lives on drugs. There were boyfriends—usually men flush enough to feed her habit for a week or two. There were jobs that involved selling drugs. There were thefts, fights, one overdose and several near-overdoses, a bout with hepatitis.

From time to time Mary Ellen would surface at the doors of "straight" friends, telling tales of reformation and exciting job possibilities, "if only I could get a little money to travel." If the friends did *not* help her, she stole from them; if they *did* help her, she stole, too, then disappeared.

All her steps led her downward. Twice, it is true, she committed herself to drug rehabilitation programs—it was that or go to jail. Each time, she remembers, "I knew the very place and the very minute I would 'score' on the day I got out." So the rehab centers provided only brief upward respites. Meanwhile, she became jumpy, developed tics, couldn't sustain a conversation. Her crimes became more frequent and more severe: she stole cars, shoplifted, "ripped off" houses and apartments. Often she was arrested and once, in a West Philadelphia parking lot, she awoke from a stupor to find herself in a squad car receiving sexual attentions from two policemen.

Still, Mary Ellen remembers kindnesses from those days. A truck driver who transported her across three states, lent her his sweater, fed her, "and didn't lay a hand on me." A pastor who told her

God was more worried about her health than her sins. Some kindnesses came from the underworld. Tammy, a black prostitute, "would always take me in." Jake, a retired man-about-town, "would let three or four crash in his living room and never take nothing." Her most affectionate memory is of a man named Red.

I met Red, still cocky, in the state penitentiary at the midpoint of his "five-to-ten"-year sentence. Since a writer's visit makes a pleasant interruption in prison routine, he was glad to talk. Throughout the interview he kept tossing his head to the right, as though still flicking aside the long red hair recently cut short by the prison barber.

I came into the bar by the Red Arrow one evening, and there she was. You could see she was on drugs, being jumpy-like. But she was a good-looking chick who reminded me of a cousin of mine: good strong body, nice laugh when she really meant to laugh. I could see she was broke, too, so I just— well, I just started taking care of her.

"Taking care of her" meant protecting a woman from assault, robbery, rape. It meant finding a place for the two of them to crash each night and always having money (or ideas for getting it) with which to keep a supply of heroin, pot, 'ludes, purple cows and what-not on hand. Red and Mary Ellen became lovers, whatever the term means for a constantly drugged-out pair. And they became partners.

Together they robbed a local drug dealer, then had to flee to another town. Once they had a "connection" who paid them $80 for every stolen car. They robbed a church, several houses, a Seven-Eleven Store. Once, to their delight, they ripped off a house that they later discovered belonged to a judge. Then they were picked up by an alert state trooper checking a license plate.

Not only did Mary Ellen kick and curse the trooper, she lied about her age and name. Her resistance landed her in the courtroom of Ralph Pickering, a tough judge who promptly packed her off for pre-trial detention to Clearfield County Jail, 165 miles away. It took her three months to establish that she was Mary Ellen and not "Lisa Smith" and that she was only eighteen and still (but barely) a minor by Pennsylvania law. Eager to get out, she became active in religious practices at the county jail. Her involvement was, she admits, "a con. I did everything I could up there to prove that butter wouldn't melt in my mouth. I was just the sweetest thing you ever saw."

Eventually Judge Pickering had her brought to his bench for release. "He told me he was letting me go this time, giving me another chance. Which I knew was a lie: he was letting me go because I was a minor and because the county had no facilities for female prisoners anyway—the place they had was too small, and they were under court order to put nobody else in it." This attitude toward the courts is not strange. It reflects what Mary Ellen had learned about figures entrusted with authority: physicians are people you buy drugs from, foster fathers try to "make it" with you, juvenile care officers don't give a damn what happens as long as everything is quiet, cops have a whack at you in the squad car and judges play the mercy bit when all they're doing is saving the county a dime.

Mary Ellen went back to Red, back to drugs, back to crime. "But I had this feeling," she says now, "that I was going to end up dead. There wasn't nothing that I was in control of; there wasn't nothing *there* in anything any more, 'cept getting high." Mary Ellen and Red had a brief burst of prosperity, writing prescriptions on a stolen book of blanks; in four days they made $3,000. They lived high on this for a week in New York. Then broke, in a dope dealer's West Side apartment, they decided, as Mary Ellen recalls, that "there just wasn't anything to do but for me to go out on the street to make a stake."

So on a February evening she went out, crossed Broadway and placed herself in the entrance alcove of a store that had just closed. Backlit by the shop windows, she must have been an appealing young figure. But, she says,

> All I could do was stand there and cry and shiver. It was so cold and I was so low. I hadn't never done this. Oh sure, I had slept with lots of guys. And usually there was some kind of exchange—I knew they'd give me drugs or dinner or a bed. But I hadn't never stood anywhere and said, "Here I am, where's your money?" So I cried and cried, and suddenly, here comes Red, running across the street against the light, and he takes my arm and says, "Let's get out of here; you can't do this—." Then I really cried.

They stole another car, headed for Pennsylvania, ran out of gas ten miles from home and were arrested along the highway. Faced with a woman who had just turned nineteen, Judge Pickering didn't fool around: "One to three," he told her. Prison at first was a ward at the county mental hospital. The county still hadn't built those needed facilities for females, and "good honest crooks" like Mary Ellen had to "put up with the crazies." After three months she finally made it to an eight-by-six, two-bed cubicle in the place where they put people who get their "just deserts."

The first three months of Mary Ellen's sentence were both wretched and busy. She was "coming down" off drugs in cold-turkey prison style. At the same time she had to win space to live—to fight off some people and avoid others, to establish herself as "somebody not to mess with." Still, she made one friend, a black streetwalker from Philadelphia.

As the drugs flushed out of Mary Ellen's system, something approaching sanity reappeared. "I found myself doing a lot of thinking," she says. "I knew I had to do something so as never to get so low again as I felt there on Broadway. I knew also that I wouldn't ever be tough enough or smart enough to stay out of trouble by myself."

The prison chaplain—a fortyish woman minister who had seen a hundred Mary Ellens come and go—paid no attention at first to the inmate in the back row. And the new Mary Ellen who made a second approach to religion didn't push herself forward. But the chaplain, sensing her loneliness, included the new woman in her rounds. Soon she gave Mary Ellen small tasks—setting up for worship, passing out hymnals, welcoming the visiting gospel teams.

For the most part, the Christians who came regularly to Mary Ellen's jail, or who visit most U.S. penitentiaries, are not Presbyterians, Methodists or Lutherans. The steady, Sunday-by-Sunday visiting is done by people whose religion is not process-oriented but event-oriented: the full gospelers, the store-front Baptists, the Pentecostals, who believe that God can touch a man or woman's heart and soul right now, and change them. Mainline denominations tend to be represented in the persons of chaplains. But apart from such chaplains, the models for understanding the gospel and living a Christian life that are presented to prisoners come from evangelical churches, assemblies and tabernacles in the United States. So Mary Ellen came to know, respect, love and eventually believe the ordinary workers who came to "witness" to prisoners, and to identify "witness" itself with their quartets, guitars, testimonies and outstretched hands.

Another form of Christian witness reentered Mary Ellen's life when, on her birthday, Perry Blaine visited the prison. He had cured himself of the rancor that he and Martha once felt for their

oster child. Thereafter Perry came regularly. Otherwise the faces
rom "outside" were few. Red, behind bars himself, sent postcards
urging Mary Ellen to keep her chin up and her nose clean.

Mary Ellen read avidly the Bible studies that her visitors gave
her and the Bible itself. She listened to gospel programs on the
radio and wrote away for booklets that the radio preachers offered.
She attended every Bible class, service and hymn-sing the prison
held. Prisoners often turn to religion in these ways, sometimes
out of need, sometimes in search of good marks for parole hearings.
But Mary Ellen soon passed beyond such self-serving behavior
to become the jailhouse evangelist. She organized her own prayer
meetings, Bible studies, counseling sessions. In part her zeal meant
that Mary Ellen was trying out faith as a core for her life in much
the same way that she had once experimented with drugs—pell-
mell, all brakes off. But this time her activities were not consciously
manipulative. It's even said that she once became enraged about
noise from an adjoining corridor during her prayer time and sallied
forth to beat up the culprit.

Mary Ellen was denied parole on her first appeal. Bitterly disappointed, she went back to her room to weep. There she found
the Philadelphia prostitute waiting to comfort her. This is the day
and the moment from which Mary Ellen, who in matters of religion
is much given to tracing days and moments, dates her soul's
salvation: "I'd been on a head trip," she says, "or maybe it was
just the Lord taking his time, getting me ready. But while 'Cele
and I sat beside each other crying, the Lord sent such a wave
of warmth and love and feelin' sure about everything over me
that I just said, 'Okay, Lord, you want me here a while longer;
I'll just stay and keep busy.'"

* * *

We have not reached the end of Mary Ellen's story when we
leave her in that prison room, on that bed, coming to terms with
her parole rejection. I am happy to report that she is free now,
and married, and a member in good standing of a mothers' group
in a store-front church not far from the town where her story
began. But stopping at the point of her parole refusal gives us
a chance to consider what an average citizen's complicity may
have been in the processes and decisions that sent a growing
child, later a woman, into that bleak, hazy country that lies beyond
the law.

Most of us have known at least one foster child; I have known several. I never took a personal interest in such a child, never considered seriously whether he or she was receiving appropriate treatment, comfort, education. I just assumed that responsibility for such matters rested somewhere else—with a court, a social worker, a foster parent. But how many people along the line of responsibility for Mary Ellen made similar assumptions? Doesn't every community have some organizations and people who ought to take an interest in these children, no matter where official responsibility lies? For example, in Mary Ellen's story the saddest line may be "She cannot remember a pastor whose interest in her survived a change of foster family." To which we might add "or a church officer or Sunday school teacher either."

Most of us are prepared, where our own sons and daughters are concerned, to incur heavy medical, psychiatric and legal expenses to prevent the kind of social and moral disintegration that marked Mary Ellen's growing up. But the record shows that we are not prepared to go so far for the cast-off or alienated children of the poor, especially (as in Mary Ellen's case) of the criminal poor. We know that a lot of money was spent on this young incorrigible. But there were always limits.

Mary Ellen was sent as a small child, for example, to a diagnostic center where she was thrown in among three to four hundred similarly disturbed youngsters. In such a setting—a place of intense stress for any child, sick or well—a truly caring community might have poured forth a program of reassurance, counseling and emotional healing in high-intensity, one-on-one encounters. Instead, children waited through hours of idleness for scheduled "interviews" with professional staff who left each evening. Or, when it was time to assign Mary Ellen's "case" to a social worker, a truly caring community might have made sure that the county employed enough social workers to keep case loads to a maximum of, say, twenty children instead of several times that many.

Why is such obviously inadequate care allowed to continue? Any child-care worker, any politician, knows the answer: because the general public is unwilling to pay enough in taxes to provide proper services. And there the matter comes down to the role of the writer and readers of this book. We are the people whose pressure on county, state and national government has led to "mass produced" care of disturbed children when we know that much, much more personal attention is needed to bring children to mature, humane adulthood.

Most of us who read this book belong to churches for which

except for funding chaplaincy programs) Jesus' strong suggestion that we visit the prisoner is a dead letter (Matthew 25:37). Instead we assume that for prisons, too, proper administration, adequate space, the comfort and physical security of inmates, and the absence of "cruel or unusual punishment" are the responsibilities of someone else—the governor, the warden or the captain of the guards. Even the task of rehabilitating prisoners we are prepared to leave to treatment officers, chaplains, and the members of fundamentalist churches who, unlike most of us, visit prisons regularly. This attitude has the aura of something cheap, something passive, something unbelieving. And it connects us with all those who can't be bothered to see what is happening to people who are removed from life among us to institutions outside the community.

At least our general attitudes are consistent: we are no more ready to construct and staff adequate prisons for adults than to build adequate diagnostic centers for juveniles. Instead, supposed economizing forces construction of warehouse facilities, which are overcrowded on the day they open and offer few chances for significant rehabilitation. As for small, staff-intensive facilities in which a significant encounter with a felon's mind, soul and value system might be possible—they are deemed too expensive, and few communities are eager to host them.

How reluctant we still are to admit a link between poverty and the kind of lawbreaking that leads to incarceration. For example, consider unemployment among black people in the U.S. In October 1986, officially measured unemployment stood at 14.4 percent of the black workforce; over 34 percent of black teenagers lacked jobs. Figures for what is called "real" unemployment (which include 8 million discouraged workers who no longer seek jobs) bring the unemployment rate for blacks to 20.8 percent of the black population (real unemployment figures for the Hispanic population are 12.2 percent). In Canada, long-term unemployment is rising. Manufacturing jobs are being lost; most new jobs are in the service sector, some of them paying very low wages. This is also happening in the U.S., so that those who do find work discover the reality that 60 percent of all new jobs created between 1979 and 1984 paid less than $7,000 a year. Dealing drugs pays better, to be sure.

When real unemployment figures are translated from statistics to high-energy youths without money standing on city street corners, we are confronted with an inescapable reason why so many young men, and in the U.S. young black men in particular, go to prison. The figures also help to explain the presence in the U.S. of several hundred thousand young women left by themselves to raise the sons and daughters of imprisoned fathers, as well as thousands of children living with relatives or foster families because their mothers are in prison.

Mary Ellen was a child of low-income parents. In the U.S. today 13.3 million children live with parents whose income is below the poverty line. They are 21.3 percent of all children in the country. In 1985, 1.1 million Canadian children, or 19.2 percent of all Canadian children, lived in low-income families (but the low income lines for these Canadian figures are set almost twice as high as the poverty-level lines used for the U.S. statistics). Some of these children are developing the antisocial habits that set Mary Ellen apart. They, too, will soon be in court, will soon be subject to the cynicism and temptations that have marred her life.

The author is one of a legion of Canadian and U.S. citizens who has left the hometown anti-drug battle to the "experts." On the list of causes for Mary Ellen's trouble, drugs may not be the leading factor. But they are important—and I was too busy, or too dignified, to dirty my hands in the struggle that might have kept drug dealers out of the community I once shared with her.

Was Mary Ellen, do you suppose, a worse offender than others in Hampshire County,[*] Pennsylvania? Does she "deserve" what she has received?

"No," says Jesus, "but unless you repent, you will all likewise perish." And somewhere on that list of citizen complicities is a civic crime or two for which people like you and I should indeed repent.

---

[*] Not the real name of the county where Mary Ellen has lived most of her life.

CHAPTER 9: The Lost Indian

"When strangers sojourn with you in your land, you shall not do them wrong. The strangers who sojourn with you shall be to you as the natives among you, and you shall love them as yourselves; for you were strangers in the land of Egypt: I am the Lord your God."
(Leviticus 19:33-34)

"Behold, at that time I will deal with all your oppressors.
And I will save the lame
   and gather the outcast,
And I will change their shame into praise. . . .
At that time I will bring you home,
   at the time when I will gather you together . . ."
      says the Lord.
(Zephaniah 3:19-20)

". . . I was a stranger and you welcomed me. . . ."
(Matthew 25:35c)

Few concepts from the Scriptures are as lovely, or as universally ignored, as the directive to show special care and kindness to the sojourner, the traveler who is with us for a while and then is gone. Some attribute this concern of Old Testament writers to folk memories recalling the early existence of the *Hibiru*, or Hebrews, as nomadic clans, "wandering Arameans." Lacking local resources, this people often found themselves at the mercy of those who possessed property and lived in fixed communities.

But it is unusual in any age for the religious obligation to protect the stranger to be fulfilled. Gypsies, Jews of the Diaspora, tinkers and peddlers of every description, refugees and exiles—all sooner or later experience ill will and oppression at the hands of more settled folk. Today, in the era of computers, charge cards, Social Security numbers and credit bureaus, we no longer post signs at city limits ordering blacks out before sundown. But we do establish ordinances that ban on-street parking after 9:30 p.m. in northern New Jersey towns or prohibit overnight parking without a permit in Chicago suburbs and West Coast communities. These effectively ban all who do not "belong"—especially transients and minorities.

Hostility to the stranger, especially to the *poor* stranger, no doubt arises partly from fear of theft and other crime and partly from economic insecurity (the age-old fear of "cheap labor"). But throughout human history, among all peoples, runs a distaste for the nomad that, anthropologists conjecture, may go back to pre-historic conflicts between hunter-gatherer tribes and the first farmers and fisher-folk. Or, others suggest, the enmity may be a kind of folk memory of clashes between different varieties of the basic human stock: i.e., between ancient peoples developing along separate but similar tracks, between Cro-Magnon and Homo sapiens groups, between the "Little People" and the incoming Celts.

Whatever its origins, fear of the stranger, the rootless one, is omnipresent among us. We offer these nomads two alternatives—settle down and become like us, or move on. In Canada and the United States, this point of view ignores not only our immigrant heritage but also the presence on our continent of hunter-gatherer folk and migratory workers, probably numbering three million or more. They include perhaps 750,000 individuals descended from those tribes of Native Americans who wandered the land in pre-colonial days (though some tribes were settled then, as many are settled now). For the most part, these great-grandchildren of the land's earliest population do not consciously follow the old ways. But in their modern history, patterns of residency and employment—Vancouver today, Fort Worth tomorrow, Chicago's Pilsen District next week—suggest that the old seasonal pull to wander continues.

Others in America's nomadic population include the migrant community (many of whose members descend from the Yaqui, Apache and other tribes of northern Mexico), about 22,000 gypsies and a minority of the Inuit folk. Still others are runaway teenagers or are ex-patients among the tens of thousands released from mental hospitals since 1965 under a law which promised but has not delivered many community treatment facilities. Young people, young families, women and psychiatric patients released from hospitals all add to the growing number of the homeless in Canada.

*   *   *

I began to take special note of the nomadic community about a year ago when a man named Jack Barker died at the age of forty-four in a San Diego "shelter for the homeless." The cause

f Jack Barker's death was pneumonia, brought on by malnutrition
nd a constitution weakened by chronic alcoholism. Such a death
s not remarkable—people perish from these causes every day,
n every city. But the passing of Jack Barker was significant to
ne because I knew him, had learned a little of his history and
vas distantly related to his people. In every generation, theirs
as been the story of the sojourner.

In the southern Indiana backcountry around Paoli, French Lick
nd Hindostan Falls live people of a physical type found only
n one or two other areas of America. Close observation reveals
 rawhide look; they tend to tallness and have long faces, shoul-
lers that are broad side-to-side but thin front-to-back, and calf
nuscles stretched long and flat against the back of the bone. The
air of people belonging to these families is universally black; their
kin is the color once called butternut. After much thought I recalled
vhere else I had seen people who looked like this: in western
North Carolina, among the Cherokees. The southern Indiana
eople are not Cherokees, however, or if they are, have long
orgotten the fact. But that they carry a strong admixture of Indian
lood there is no doubt, although it is only in this generation
hat they have begun to admit to, let alone boast of, the ancestors
n a grandparent's side who belonged to "The People." The near
bsence of organized Indian groups in Indiana and Illinois today
uggests that the region's original Miami, Illinois and Shawnee
nhabitants were killed, driven out or found it wise to submerge
hemselves in the culture of the newcomers. But that was long
go.

Into one of these clans, the Barkers,* the infant later named
ack entered at birth in 1942. His name recalled his mother's brother,
who had gone off years before to work in an oilfield. The Barkers
vere well-known, sometimes infamous, in the area. In the
nineteenth century a band of them, dubbed "The Barker Gang"
n sheriff's posters, robbed travelers on trains and highways. Gang
members survived hanging only in a photograph; they too had
ack's "Cherokee" look.

As a child Jack liked to hunt and was a fairly good hand on
a farm run by his uncle. But with school and studies Jack held
no truck. A teacher remembers that "he was not unintelligent,
but he was certainly inattentive." There is no evidence that he
finished the eighth grade.

---

* None of the names of people in this chapter are real names.

Jack disappeared from home when he was fifteen. The fami briefly considered sending the police after him. But Mary Bark recalls that "he was already a big boy, maybe six foot tall, an strong, and we figgered he could look out for himself." Burie in that easy phrase is the family memory of the boys in ever generation who left home early and were indeed able to "loo out for themselves."

Every couple of years, Jack showed up at home, usually in tim for a marriage, a death—some big family event. Nobody coul figure out how he knew when to come, since nobody was eve sure just where he was, and he never telephoned ahead. But o any day when the family needed to be complete, Jack would appea

A cousin's wedding was one such occasion. He came late t the ceremony, wore brown trousers and jacket, and sat agains the wall during the reception. Afterwards, asking themselves wha Jack had talked about, the family concluded: "Nothing." He came he sat, he was "together" with all the family he had, and afte lingering a few days more with his brother, he departed.

We heard from Jack at intervals over the years. Like his long disappeared uncle, he worked for a while in the oilfields, the on a drilling rig in the Gulf of Mexico. Then he was in Dalla for a while, in New York, in Spokane. Once a landlady in Bartlesvill called to say that he was sick. There were interminable conference about just who should go down to Oklahoma to sit with Jac through the illness. By the time the family reached a decisio and called the landlady back, Jack had recovered and gone.

Oldtimers in the Barker clan will tell you that every generatio has had its Jack—the quiet, taciturn one, the dreamer with dee affections and a dreadful temper lurking just beneath the silence and an itchy foot. But not until I visited Pine Ridge in the Dakota did I learn, from long conversations with Jack Tootoosis and othe Indian friends, that there is a "Jack" in many Plains Indian families Indeed, so many rovers have come from these tribes that some outsiders have speculated about a special illness, a kind of Native American schizophrenia, that must account for the withdrawal the reserve, the inevitable wandering off to other places. This i nonsense, of course: what we have here is a remnant, a collective memory of some kind, of the days when camp was struck each time the herds moved or the seasons changed.

*   *   *

While all this is of great interest—at least to me—what matters in our story is not why our two nations have so many people who must travel from place to place, but what happens to them when they do. Because what happens to them is a shame and a disgrace.

Remember that this is the age of the document. If a police officer stops you on the highway, the first request is that you establish your identity. But the signs of our identities that please the law are proofs of roots and relationships: a Social Security card, a credit card, a tax receipt, a voter's registration card. A nomad has no such proofs. Exercising the North American's first social and economic right, freedom to travel, requires a driver's license. But who ever saw a driver's license marked "no fixed address"? So for a traveling worker, a nomad, to be stopped by police anywhere is to be hassled, detained and forced to call somebody, somewhere.

Remember too that this is the age of sky-high medical bills and hospitals that demand proof of ability to pay before a broken leg can be set. It is true that all the oil companies and some growers provide medical coverage for their workers. But what happens if a picker is injured while traveling from one job to another or develps a malady that is not job-related?*

Finally, what happens to the wanderer when no work is to be found? Unemployment insurance was designed for the settled worker, the resident of a particular state or county. It does not apply to the seasonal laborer. In many states in the U.S., public assistance is all but barred to unemployed, able-bodied males; even unemployed women have trouble qualifying for allowances unless children are involved. A nomad has no chance at all for such aid. The situation is like that commented on by a Canadian who works with the homeless in Ontario: "If the homeless can't get welfare unless they have an address, how do they ever get enough money to rent a place and get an address?"

With his oilfield worker's skills, Jack Barker had steadier, better-paying jobs in his lifetime than do most nomads. Nevertheless, his "career" ran counter to the North American success-story pattern: decreasing employability as his health collapsed, jobs held for increasingly shorter periods, eventual relegation to derelict's row, death. Yet to the end, Jack had some advantages: there were

---

* More than 50.7 million United States citizens who lack health insurance can answer the question, and their answers are one long tale of treatment denied, humiliation exacted, dignity desecrated. In addition, Medicaid covers only 50 percent of people living at poverty level. See the Appendix for further information.

people whom he could call for a loan, for identification, for a place to go when he wanted to. Many have no such recourse.

Mark one fact well: for many migrants, many nomads, there is time in jail. Sometimes the charge is simple vagrancy. Sometimes no charge exists: "pending investigation," reads the blotter. That such detention is illegal matters little when you are stopped in one of those small tank towns marked on the plains and the local police want time to check back through the records. But sometimes the charges are real; some migrants, when broke, do shoplift, do try to cheat the clerk at the gas pump, do hawk some nonexistent scheme or shoddy product. Others keep the hunter-gatherers' custom of the feast—a binge and a steak dinner on payday, broke tomorrow.

Today the United Farmworkers are busy organizing migrant farmworkers. Sooner or later the industry will be regulated, conditions will improve, wages and benefits will rise. Sooner or later also, mechanization will replace the last of the manual labor jobs at oil wells, the last deckhand's job on a ship, the last off-loading job in the produce yards.

None of these changes will end the day of the nomads. Some people will continue to move across the land because they must travel to find work. And others, like the unregistered, unrecognized semi-Indian of this chapter, will travel in response to some deep, inward, culture-rooted call of ancient ways. What sort of reception will these people receive in our towns?

When the shelter sent Jack Barker's belongings home to Paoli, Indiana, the family found a lot of outlandish items in the bag. There were pay stubs from a dozen states, fifteen packs of matches from places as far south as Guatemala, a receipt for a "drunk and disorderly" fine paid to a court, a paperback about the old Barker gang, and a photograph in old-fashioned sepia of Jack's sister at her high school graduation.

I was in the room when Evelyn Barker Baxter saw that photo of herself. She shed a tear and said, "I sure hope most people were good to him, along the way."

But she knew it wasn't so.

PART II: Face to Face, Hand to Hand

And the multitudes asked John, "What then shall we do?"
And he answered them, "Let anyone who has two coats
share with the one who has none; and let the one who has
food do likewise."
    (Luke 3:10-11)

If a brother or sister is ill-clad and in lack of daily food, and
one of you says to them, "Go in peace, be warmed and
filled," without giving them the things needed for the body,
what does it profit?
    (James 2:15-16)

CHAPTER 10: What a Church Can Do

> At present . . . I am going to Jerusalem with aid for the saints. For Macedonia and Achaia have been pleased to make some contribution for the poor among the saints at Jerusalem; they were pleased to do it, and indeed they are in debt to them, for if the Gentiles have come to share in their spiritual blessings, they ought also to be of service to them in material blessings.
>
> (Romans 15:25-27)

By now, readers of *Breach of Promise* will be asking themselves what a congregation can do to mend the breach that cuts the poor off from the promises we claim should be for all. Perhaps the best beginning is to examine briefly what church members should *not* do.

Last year an adolescent boy in a northern New Jersey town committed suicide. There seemed to have been no reason for him to take his life: he was healthy, intelligent, and belonged to a family quite able financially to give him a good start in life. In a note found with his body, the teenager had written, "There is so much sorrow in the world, and I can't do anything about it."

Succumbing to depression or cynicism, as an individual or a group, is *not* the way to start easing the burdens of poverty. Although Moses' prediction that "the poor will never cease out of the land" (Deuteronomy 15:11) continues to prove true, it would be sinful to permit the somber fact of human suffering to deny us the joys of life—of being alive, of meeting new and interesting people, of appreciating one another. That no one today can wave a wand to wipe out suffering in the world and in our own communities is no reason, ever, for ceasing to hail the rise of God's sun every morning.

Sometimes I have felt that people in some traditionally poor communities in America realize this simple truth better than more prosperous folk. In early childhood, at least, some children of an urban ghetto or of a Native American community appear to be freer and happier than overprotected youngsters from suburban neighborhoods. I'm not sure why this is so, but I believe it is because the parents of the poorer youngsters have learned to cherish laughter more than property. If true, this is a trait worth emulating.

Recognize what we owe one another

In addition to living as people confident of God's goodness toward creation, we also need to recapture as individuals and as congregations the sense of being in debt to each other—each person in debt to every other person, each group in debt to every other group, and all this indebtedness stemming from our common origin in God and from the shared new life that we owe to the work of Jesus Christ. It is this sense of mutual obligation that Paul lifts up in the verses at the head of this chapter.

From such an understanding developed the political concept of the *commonwealth*, incorporated by American revolutionaries into the documents that defined and established the United States. This concept, derived from the term "common weal" current in sixteenth-century England, once was used widely by Christians to mean something close to "the reign of God." In its secular use, it has come to refer to all the people, to the body politic, and especially to associations of citizens or states. Canada and other nations that have a similar original relationship to Britain view a commonwealth as extending far beyond one nation.

The early political leaders of the U.S. interpreted the commonwealth concept in widely different ways. But all at least paid lip service to the notion, some invested great passion in it, and together they let it stand as one of three or four principles at the heart of their dream of a new nation. The subsequent history of the U.S., like that of other democracies (as well as of nations still striving to become more democratic) can be seen as the struggle of previously excluded groups of people to be truly included in this common dream.

Honor what the poor contribute

The reality of our indebtedness to each other goes far beyond political history. We have continually drawn from one another's cultures. Without contributions from all our races, nationalities and religious traditions, there would be no true North American music, art, literature or law. The same can be said of our economies: no major North American fortune or industry exists that does not have its roots somewhere in the slave trade, in manufacturing that depended in some way on the work of slaves, or in the availability of such low-wage workers as are found among immigrant groups. Some industries—especially food production, auto-making, fishing, construction—have required a pool of unemployed persons available for seasonal work. And every bit of this development rests on the sacrifice exacted from the Native American population: their enforced displacement from a hunter-gatherer way of life or their removal from settled areas so that a continent could be released to newcomers.

Look for global consequences

Parenthetically, we also need to realize that today's global economy demands similar sacrifices on an intercontinental scale. Thus, New England shoemakers are thrown out of work by an agreement between governments that allows the United States to import Korean-made shoes if the Koreans refrain from making microchips. Similarly, Indian farmers in Guatemala find themselves forced from their traditional cornfields when the owners put such fields to grass in order to raise beef for North American hamburgers.

Not only have North America's poor been among the cultural and economic shapers of our societies, they have also been among the first to defend those societies. North America has never had "gentlemen's wars"; in times of conflict the humbler people have always been called to make the nations' greatest sacrifices. They have done this willingly, for the most part, and even enthusi-astically. Perhaps this is why those who did most of the fighting and dying on behalf of the United States in its war in Vietnam were black, Native American, or white youths from small towns and rural areas, while the sons of more comfortable citizens were more likely to stay secure behind educational draft deferments.

Begin to make good on our debts

So as Christians who are about to investigate what our churches can do, we consult our memories and draw upon personal experiences of poverty. We ponder our mutual indebtedness, with gratitude toward the multitude of known and unknown people who have helped us to become what we are. Then, conscious that we "have come to share in spiritual blessings" as a result of the sacrifices of those among us who are poor, we can move with energy and intelligence to consider how we may "be of service to them in material blessings," so that promises now broken may in justice be fulfilled.

And now as members of a congregation, we know of a family or person in trouble in our town;[*] we wish to act from our faith and our sense of interdependence to assist that family or that person. What do we do next?

Respond to a specific local situation

We first learn all we can. What is the problem with which that person or family must deal? What are the most important elements of the problem? What is the timetable that leads to catastrophe for the family or person—how long until the house is lost, or creditors institute legal action, or unemployment compensation runs out, or a needed operation becomes impossible? Of course, much of this sensitive information must come from the person or family themselves, so we must be sensitive about who gathers the information and how it is used (see suggestions at the end of Chapter Seven). And our means of helping must always support the goal of assisting a person or family to make their own best decisions.

We must ask ourselves, very seriously and realistically, what resources are available to us to help a person with his or her difficulty. Sometimes the thing needed is entirely within our grasp—the extra few hundred dollars in our checking account, or the lawyer in town who owes us a favor, or the college that just might, if a persistent graduate made the need known, have a scholarship for an unemployed parent's child. If so, our task is relatively easy: write the check, call the lawyer, get in touch with the school. And then, in a way that preserves self-respect as far as possible, get word to the person or family concerned that help is on the way.

Work through the congregation

More frequently, the need we hope to meet goes beyond our personal resources. In such instances, resist the "give what you can and get out" approach. To offer a family $250 when it needs $28,000 is not only to give far too little but to put the recipients in an awkward position—since they cannot rejoice over your gift as they feel they should, they incur ingratitude that adds to their

---

[*] I refer here to the kind of trouble that is financial or at least has an economic component—which, as we have seen, covers a wide spectrum of situations. But some of these next steps could be used when a church wishes to assist people with problems that stem from other causes.

hopelessness. Instead, knowing that we cannot personally meet a need ought to send us back to our local church to ask ourselves some hard questions.

Most of those questions concern the congregation to which we belong. In preparing to seek congregational help for others, we must ask where—in what organization or group, formal or informal—is this congregation's real center for service. Almost every church has a committee for mission service—some call it a Board of Deacons, some a Christian Service Committee, others a Stewards' Committee. But in some congregations these groups have degenerated into bodies that do little more than see that the flowers in the chancel are distributed after the service. If this is the case, one must go through or beyond the mission service unit to the congregation's central governing board to discover whether funds can be unlocked for emergency services. Remember that someone seeking emergency help usually has no time to try to expand a committee's or board's sense of mission responsibility: catastrophe will strike a suffering person or family while some members of the targeted committee are still mulling over their inhibitions or recovering from disinterest. Remember, too, that your church's pastor not only has a right to know what you are trying to accomplish within the congregation, but that he or she will also want to help you. Your pastor can often open up committee agendas faster than you can. And most pastors have a small fund at their disposal that may prove a useful start toward your goal.

Involve ecumenical and service groups

If, as may be, neither a church group nor the church as a whole has resources to meet the need that challenges you, go to your pastor again and outline the difficulty. Seek his or her help—or blessing, if for some reason the pastor cannot become personally involved—in making further approaches to possible sources of funds and other help in your community. Such moments are a church member's best opportunity to experience the joys (and the frustrations) of the ecumenical movement by getting in touch with other churches, church councils, and other ecumenical bodies. Also, don't forget the service clubs in your town, the local family- or health-care agencies, the United Way, and so on.

Most of us require the support of a recognized institution when we seek allies for solving problems of individuals, problems that so quickly take on social dimensions. In approaches to social service agencies, it will help immensely if you can make it known that your church and pastor are behind your effort. Nevertheless, you may finally need to form a new group to address the problem faced by your needy neighbor. At this point, matters become delicate indeed. Two considerations are especially important:

First, be sure that you are not "reinventing the wheel" by duplicating a service that already exists. Get out the telephone directory for your community and for the nearest metropolitan area. Check county and city service listings. In the Yellow Pages (or business directory) check under appropriate topical indexes for nearby organizations designed to intervene in situations similar to the one you are trying to address. If such a group exists, call and ask for assistance. In addition, a bewildering array of national organizations will help people organize to meet specific challenges. These range down the alphabet from "A"—for "Alzheimer's Disease"—to "Z"—for the "Promotion and Support of Zoological Gardens." Some organizations frequently contacted for information and assistance in issues related to poverty are listed in the Appendix of this book.

Keep confidences, respect privacy

Second, in all that you do, keep in mind the right to privacy of those whom you are seeking to serve. Remember that the first thing many people do when they fall into serious personal or economic trouble is to stop attending church—the Sunday after a business fails, for example. At the least such an action shows a troubled person's concern to tend to his or her pain in solitude; at worst it says a great deal about how the church community is perceived in times of trouble. Therefore, the last thing you want to do, as someone who wants to help, is to turn a family's misfortune into a topic of common gossip.

In regard to concern for pride and privacy, your integrity and motivation in trying to help someone are very much on the line, and can be destroyed or preserved depending on your cautiousness in selecting potential members of your group. Try to make your list of approachable people realistic: if you need to raise $10,000 to help, there is no point listing ten people if six of those ten are only a paycheck away from public assistance themselves. But once you have made your list, proceed as follows:

a) Ask your pastor, or a friendly banker, to hold the money as you obtain it.

b) Call each person on your list and ask for all or part of what is needed. Do *not* make any assumptions about how much anyone should give, but *do* make sure that everyone knows both the total amount required and the number of people you intend to approach.

At this point, many people object that they cannot "ask for money, ever." The answer is that "Yes, you can!"—as long as you have given from your resources in the same proportion that you are asking neighbors to give from theirs. If your cause is a just one, and if you have chosen to approach people who also recognize the interdependence that ought to pervade Christian society, you will get what is needed from those on your list, or enough of it to justify continuing in your quest. What's more, you will create a circle of friends who will be linked with you at a deeper spiritual level than you have ever known before, because working together in a service of mercy leads to just such a result.

Gather the community to meet its needs

Most of these steps have focussed on raising money for someone in trouble. Actually, money isn't always, or even usually, at the core of what is needed. Reflect for a moment on the story from Allerton, Iowa, told in Chapter Five. It was certainly not within the power of farmer-pastor Ross Blount to find money to save the farms of his elders. The actions he and Lorena could take fell into three categories:

1. They could "open up" the topic of going broke on the farm, taking it from the shadow of fear and shame to the sunlight of open discourse. People could then talk about their situations and discover a community of support that can be enjoyed even in times of trouble.
2. They could summon people to find the strength of their inner resources—with the Day of Prayer that Lorena started, for example, or the Men's Bible Club begun by Ross.
3. They could connect farm families in their congregations to other people and organizations trying to find solutions for the farm crisis.

These three examples of action illustrate the kind of ministry that brings people in poverty together to support one another, to provide immediate help for some who need it and to promote understanding of the causes of poverty so that they can be challenged and changed. The farm crisis is not the only kind of economic desperation affecting millions of lives in North America (we will not try to rank such desperation and suffering). But the responses to the family farm crisis by different congregations, persons and communities can serve us here as models of what churches can do. Examining such models can lead us to develop the most appropriate responses in our own communities, whether the problem is homelessness, inadequate public assistance, a plant closing, the need of single parents for good child care, or another problem. So these farm communities provide examples for us all.

Assess community strengths and limits

If we go east from Allerton to the even smaller Iowa community of Lone Tree, we see the same three functions of ministry operating in a similar situation. In Lone Tree farmers are also going broke, and the tiny Lone Tree congregation, led by a pastor named Al Best, also cannot hope to put things together again financially for farmers.

Like the Blounts, Al Best knows the people of his farm community very well. Early in the unfolding farm crisis, he noted that intense feelings of failure and shame among hard-pressed farmers prevented them from consulting counseling services in the Lone Tree area. So the pastor made sure that word went round the congregation that meetings, seminars and counseling services dealing with the farm crisis were available at the county seat, a larger town within driving distance. And he posted at church a list of psychiatrists in communities at a suitable remove from Lone Tree.

Lone Tree's church also kept a watchful eye on community youth during this time of trouble. In Lone Tree, as in Allerton, farm couples kept the news of their financial condition from their children, so the loss of family farms fell like bombshells on young lives. The Lone Tree youngsters felt the effects of the crisis in their parents' shortened tempers, deteriorating marriages, greater use of alcohol and so on, long before they learned the facts of the situation. Honest discussions of the farm crisis in the schools, which began partly at the insistence of the Bests, did much to defuse the hostility toward parents that the parents' own behavior, left unexplained, might otherwise have caused.

It is worth noting that careful attention to church members' needs during a crisis will not protect the congregation from its full share of the pain that comes with tragedy. Thus, on one grim morning, Al Best was awakened by a phone call from a distraught mother who told him that her son had murdered his banker. In the hours that followed, the pastor, struggling with the mother's grief and his own dismay, nevertheless was able to feel that the burden was somehow lighter because the church had at least tried to prevent such worst outcomes.

Realize the power of a motivated person

Sometimes a significant movement can be set in motion by one person's passion to help. Not long ago *U.S. News and World Report* featured the story of Rita Hennig, of Tekamah, Nebraska. After her own farm had failed, Mrs. Hennig formed the Heartland Crisis Food Pantry to feed hard-pressed families. Today seventy families whose pride will not permit them to take food stamps feed their families, at least in part, from the food pantry. Or consider Sandra Simonson. Having lost her farm, she set out to create Wisconsin's "Project HOPE" ("Help Our People Endure"), a group that provides emotional support to suffering families with the idea that if people "talk out" their fears and anxieties, they will be less likely to express them by suicide or violence. In this connection, we recall once more that almost everyone who experiences an economic disaster enters, at some early point, a period of self-imposed isolation. Mrs. Simonson remembers that when her children went to school, she would tell them, "Now don't you talk to anyone about our family problems." Similarly, a woman whose husband recently died of a heart attack—attributed by her to foreclosure on the family farm—remembers that "the hardest part was going back to church." To break through to such people is not easy. It is not enough that programs of aid exist; one must ensure that such programs are placed in front of troubled people so they cannot ignore them.

Count on those with experience

Often the best way to approach a difficult problem affecting a community is through a person who is included in the trouble. After all, the best kind of development remains self-development. Mary Noland, of Adair, Iowa, is a farmer who is still in business but struggling to survive. Nevertheless, she has found time amid her own hardships to consider the condition of neighbors who are worse off than she. The first thing that Mary Noland did for her neighbors (after the obvious impulse to start a food and clothing closet) was to establish a farm women's support group. The group has since grown to a circle of fifteen to twenty women who meet weekly to talk through their concerns. Next Mrs. Noland started a couple's support group. Most recently, she has arranged for visits to her community by mental health professionals, counselors in developing alternative skills and income, and so on. It is no wonder, then, that the Presbytery of Des Moines, desiring to get a "handle" on how to help beleaguered farm families, has created an Emergency Aid Fund, administered through Mary Noland, which ensures that when worse comes to worst, no one in the Adair area goes hungry. Area offices of other denominations have similar stories to share.

Extend the network

Often working through denominational links, churches in the farm belt have done much to assist family farmers. In Nebraska the Farm Crisis Network, funded by a long list of Catholic and Protestant bodies, is a state-wide organization that provides financial, emotional, legal, medical, housing (utility costs, weather-proofing) and food services to impoverished families. One feature of the operation is the Farm Crisis Hotline, a counseling service whose telephone usually rings when a farm wife first realizes that her husband is in deeper financial trouble than he is willing to admit to himself or to her. On the receiving end of the Hotline, a staff person sits listening, assessing each situation as it is related. The data is then passed on to a field worker who may call on the family, offering the network's many services.

Similar help is provided by such organizations as the Iowa Inter-Church Agency for Peace and Justice, the Kansas Interfaith Rural Aid Committee, the Louisiana Interchurch Farm Crisis Coalition, the Minnesota Council of Churches, the Prairie Fire Rural Action Coalition, the National Catholic Rural Life Congress, the Federation of Southern Cooperatives/Land Assistance Fund, rural life programs and emphases in several Canadian denominations, and many other groups. The Rural Crisis Issue Team of the National Council of Churches Division of Church and Society has taken a lead in coordinating such efforts and has disbursed more than $1.25 million in thirty-two U.S. states to help start relief and assistance efforts.

Recognize risks when trying to change systems

Sooner or later in every aid effort, some people—like Ross Blount, in Allerton, for example—start to wonder whether the root causes of poverty should be addressed. Nothing is harder than winning agreement on this question, especially when the causes are not single factors but are woven into a whole economic and political system involving shifts and trends beyond the capacity of single persons or groups to affect. Thus, in churches in the Midwest, there is a will to help suffering farmers by providing food, counseling, and relocation aid. But there is no consensus about the lengths to which a person or organization may go to protect the family farm.

When such major policy issues divide well-meaning people, one has two basic choices: either to find or form a group of people willing to push for solutions through legislative reform, lobbying and public protest, or to settle for doing what one can for one's neighbors. Short-term efforts are *not* contemptible, as anyone who has ever been homeless or hungry will readily attest. Therefore, when a farm area church provides counseling or when a downtown church opens its doors to provide temporary shelter to homeless people, their members may indeed take satisfaction—by which I mean spiritual satisfaction—in their work.

Few churches with such bread-and-butter ministries would claim to be ameliorating the bedrock reasons why people are homeless, farmless, jobless, or cast adrift. And when a Ross Blount mobilizes church members to plant crosses on the courthouse lawn to dramatize the human cost of foreclosures, or when farmers themselves picket offices in Washington, the controversy created by these public actions may actually erode some of the support available for short-term assistance, as well as for the future. So in seeking to make assistance effective, groups must walk a fine line when moving beyond immediate aid to witness for eradicating the causes of poverty.

Practice creative compassion

When helping people, there is always room for imagination. One Georgia church has a long tradition of opening its doors in times of need. Like a lot of other churches, it runs a night helter for the homeless. But it has taken a creative look *downward*. Someone has thought about the feet of people who wander the street during the day looking for work. So this church has arranged for regular podiatric care at the shelter, a service whose necessity seems obvious once one has seen it in operation. Here, too, in a kind of ministry that many churches already practice, the building is opened as headquarters and meeting space for volunteer groups dedicated to special causes.

Specialize for particular needs

One of the best reasons for beginning a specialized ministry in your church is because "nobody else seems interested." One area that never has enough "interested" people is prison ministry. This truly compassionate work involves personal visits to prisoners and the task of providing the all-important reentry to the community that is necessary for those who are coming out of prison. Sometimes, as in the case of the young woman whose story we told in Chapter Eight, gospel teams that visit prisons expand their work to include such risky and time-demanding ministries as running bail-bond programs or finding temporary homes, jobs and much-needed counseling for released prisoners. More often they do not. These needs go unmet, for the most part, despite valiant efforts by the Pennsylvania Prison Society and similar groups to encourage programs to meet them (see the Appendix). This area of social need, which is tied to poverty in direct and indirect ways, issues a great challenge to tough-minded but spiritually awakened Christians.

Here are a few examples of congregational involvement; look for others near your own location. The Christian Connection, involving a number of churches in Ontario, organizes discussion sessions at the Niagara Regional Detention Centre. Open to all prisoners, these "rap groups" range in subject from current events to moral issues to coping with life both in and out of prison. With church help, a contractor in Alabama has set in motion an employment program for released prisoners. A congregation near the famous prison in Ossining, New York, has added an associate pastor to its staff for the sole purpose of working at the huge institution with inmates and their families. And in Brooklyn, New York, a new church—called Gethsemane Church—has been chartered by its denomination. Its members are former prisoners, their families, and those who take an interest in their lives.

Seek direction from the community

Finally, let us return to that used clothing cupboard—"Any Garment, Ten Cents"—that we saw in Racine, West Virginia. Over the years Racine has received a good deal of church money through self-development projects, small business loans, housing rehabilitation grants, and so on. The results of these have mostly faded, sometimes leaving little more than a flaking coat of once-fresh paint on aging structures of no great initial value anyway. One of the reasons these well-intentioned projects failed is because they did not begin with local initiative but were, instead, someone else's idea of what was needed. The small used-clothing store is different: a local woman began it and made the necessary contacts in Charleston, the nearest city large enough to provide sizable contributions. She administers the clothing service herself with the help of neighbor women. The little undertaking is rooted in the community; for this reason, it endures.

The Racine project exemplifies a great principle. To mend the breach of promises that causes poverty, one must begin by knowing and valuing those who are experts in poverty because of experience. People who are themselves poor can set the direction for what is needed, and we who feel challenged to help can then join in a process of realizing dreams that will become shared visions during days of working together.

As with small matters, so with large. In the next chapter we will see how a group of Christians addressed a need beyond the capacities of any single person, church or denomination to meet. The group was successful surely because its members were rooted in a community where housing was a primary need.

CHAPTER 11: Straw for the Bricks of Brooklyn: The Nehemiah Project

Pharaoh commanded the taskmasters of the people and their foremen, "You shall no longer give the people straw to make bricks, as heretofore; let them go and gather straw for themselves. But the number of bricks which they made heretofore you shall lay upon them, you shall by no means lessen it. . . .

So the people were scattered abroad throughout all the land of Egypt, to gather stubble for straw. The taskmasters were urgent, saying, "Complete your work, your daily task, as when there was straw." And the foremen of the people of Israel, whom Pharaoh's taskmasters had set over them, were beaten. . . .

Then the foremen of the people of Israel came and cried to Pharaoh, "Why do you deal thus with your servants? No straw is given to your servants, yet they say to us, 'Make bricks!' And behold, your servants are beaten; but the fault is in your own people." (Exodus 5:6-16 *passim*)

To this point, most of the responses to poverty that we have encountered have been started in behalf of, rather than by, afflicted persons or communities. When planning is good and luck present, such efforts may ameliorate social or economic hardships, but they seldom affect underlying causes. To get "at" these underlying causes, afflicted people often must act together on their own behalf.

In the Book of Exodus we read of an event that took place about 1,300 years before the birth of Christ. This report is one of the earliest references to the exercise of a basic human right, that of a people "peaceably to assemble, and to petition the Government for a redress of grievances" (as the First Amendment to the U.S. Constitution states it).

During this period of their sojourn in Egypt, the people of Israel were undergoing torment—slavery at the hands of the Egyptians. In the slave communities at the time, a man named Moses was emerging as a spokesperson, though the period of his greatest influence was yet to come. Then came a day when the Egyptians changed the work rules for the Israelites, making them glean their own straw for the bricks they were forced to manufacture. The new rule was set forth in response to Moses and Aaron's request for a three-day respite to allow the people time to worship their God.

In return the foremen of the Israelite work crews went to the Egyptian king to protest. The Pharaoh became exceedingly angry, as high authorities are wont to do when challenged by people of lesser rank. For a time the slaves' situation was made worse than before. Nevertheless, the visit proved useful. The Israelite leaders gained experience with the character of Pharaoh—learned what could be expected of him and how he would react to future challenges. More important, their own attitudes changed: they briefly blamed Moses for creating the climate that caused the king's negative reaction to their visit (people often blame their leaders for acts of oppression committed by others; see Exodus 5:20). But in the end, the visit with Pharaoh became a factor in the people's decision to follow Moses out of Egypt to Sinai.

The struggle to reclaim a community

In our time, too, afflicted people must sometimes confront authority en masse if they are to gain attention, resources and a fair deal. In the sixties, we in the U.S. witnessed the painful struggle through which blacks, with allies in the larger community, confronted public authority to claim long-denied rights. The struggle still continues in this decade, as we will see if we visit a chain of communities in East Brooklyn, New York, and look at the situation of a family like that of Lydia and Angel Torres.

To get the flavor of Brownsville in East Brooklyn, one must walk west on Blake Street, avoiding pursesnatchers and crack-crazies. A few shattered buildings remain on the rubble-strewn lots of Blake Street; all else is desolation. Yet the landscape changes when one rounds the corner onto Mother Gaston Boulevard. First, small shops appear. Although not much to look at, they are clearly conducting a vigorous trade. Next come nests of public housing. These multistory units have been up for two or three decades; the trees in their courtyards are three stories high, and someone is keeping graffiti under considerable control. Finally, after the public housing ends, one enters a neighborhood of new and attractive two-story row homes, more than 800 of them, with an additional 200 or so scheduled for completion within six months.

No signboards announce that these homes were built with

federal, state or city assistance. The only "signs"—all proclaiming "owner occupied"—are the tiny but immaculate lawns still green in early winter, the chrysanthemums and three-foot arborvitae springing from well-tended soil, and the variety of awnings, fences and gateposts (one crowned with concrete lions rampant) that testify to the purchasers' taste, industry, and freedom of innovation.

New homes with a biblical name

These houses—built by something called the "Nehemiah Project"—are the only low-income mass housing built in New York City since Congress and Ronald Reagan pulled the plug on public housing funds more than five years ago. The two- and three-bedroom brick dwellings cost $53,000 each to build; they are sold for $43,000 (a $10,000 interest-free second mortgage is payable to New York City upon resale). Each house has been occupied immediately on completion—has had to be, given the ubiquity of thieves prepared to strip plumbing and fixtures from vacant structures—by a family whose name was next on a waiting list exceeding 4,000. Purchasers usually are members of the black or Hispanic majority communities in the Brownsville area. They earn between $15,000 and $25,000 per household, and have managed to save or borrow $5,000 for a down payment.

Turning in at 426 Christopher Street, we enter the Nehemiah home belonging to Lydia and Angel Torres and their four children. They have been here four months, after a two-year wait. Angel remembers when he first heard from a friend that "the churches"—yes, that's right, the churches—were going to build houses in Brownsville. At the time he and the family were living in a large apartment building in the Flatbush area of Brooklyn. "It was terrible," he recalls. "The kids were like birds in a cage. They couldn't go out and play, and were not safe in the corridors. We were desperate to get out of that place, and afraid. We needed a house, but on our incomes [Angel's job is in a hospital; Lydia's, in the garment industry] it was not possible to dream. . . ."

Churches are centers for survival

Then came the rumor about the churches and the houses. Angel took Lydia to the building site—which looked as bombed-out as Blake Street does today. "The place was like a war, everything falling down or already gone," he says. "Lydia started to cry. She said to me, 'Man, you are crazy, to think of coming here.' But

I told her that all this is going to change. That there is a vision. . . ."

The vision came to reality. But how did it happen? And what happened to the Torres family when it came?

The story begins with desolation in the area. For three decades the nearly bankrupt City of New York gave old Brooklyn neighborhoods low priority when allocating budgets for redevelopment and services. Streets went unrepaired, and century-old pipes and cables rusted away. Old residents and old industries fled. Crime, narcotics and prostitution flourished. Just about the only community institutions left functioning were the churches. Of these, black and storefront Hispanic congregations were increasing in number and sometimes in size, but the old, mostly white Catholic and Protestant churches were emptying fast.

A few Christians begin to dream

Against this background, a Lutheran pastor, John Heinemeir, convened a group of Catholic and Protestant clergy and laity on April 6, 1978, to discuss ways that churches and their members could address area problems. The handful of people present heard about the work being done in the adjacent Borough of Queens by an organization centered on the churches. Encouraged by what they learned, the East Brooklyn group agreed to meet again. At their third meeting, on June 8, members of the group, now grown to forty clergy and laypersons, were led in discussion by Edward T. Chambers of the Industrial Areas Foundation (IAF).

The encounter between Chambers and the Brooklyn group was fortuitous for both. The Industrial Areas Foundation has its own history, beginning under radical community organizer Saul Alinsky in the Chicago of the 1940s and continuing with Chamber's emergence as Alinsky's heir in struggles with Kodak in Rochester (1965-67) and elsewhere. On the June evening when Chambers first spoke to the East Brooklyn Churches' action group, IAF had eighteen affiliated community organizations across the country and had just moved its headquarters to the New York metropolitan area. Chambers needed another local client to help meet expenses of the new office, and the Brownsville group seemed promising. In turn, Chambers' usefulness to the Brownsville group was equally related to their self-interest. One who was present recalls, "We didn't know anything except that nothing was to be expected in solving our community problems from anybody but ourselves, and Chambers was just the man to tell us how much it was going to cost."

Financing starts with congregations

What Ed Chambers told the church people was that their community amounted to "a bunch of rubble," and that their problem was one "I wouldn't touch unless you raise $200,000 to get started." He pointed them toward the upper echelons of their denominations as places to begin a funding drive, insisting at the same time that the group set up a system of dues for member congregations that would cost each, depending upon size, from $500 to $3,000 a year.

"I agreed to help them a little in raising the money," Chambers reports, adding that "the United Church of Christ's Board of Homeland Ministries took the first risk, putting up $45,000."

The new organization raised the required $200,000 in front money from denominations and from their own members (local contributions, mostly from the congregations, totalled $13,000). But in many ways, money-raising know-how was the least of what the fledgling group drew from Ed Chambers. "The man kept us in touch with reality," Lutheran pastor Dave Benke remembers, "and with our anger. He insisted that our people, pastors included, should be trained in organizing skills. He demanded that we research every project or issue to be addressed. And he made us practice ahead of time for every important meeting or 'action.'"

Once, Benke recalls, he became angry at Chambers. "He stood up there and kept telling us, again and again all evening long, that we were living in a garbage heap. Now, you really have to hear that sometimes—your mind tends to close things out just to survive, and you don't *see* anymore, after a while, what is around you. But on that night I had just come from a hospital where I visited a woman, a parishioner, who had been bound, raped, robbed and set afire in her apartment by two thieves. Somehow she still lived, trussed up in a hospital on a spit that kept turning her like a fowl so that unguents could be applied. On that night I didn't need Chambers to talk about garbage."

An ecumenical group starts to grow

Despite Chambers' constant reminders that the East Brooklyn pastors and church members confront their condition directly and soberly, the numbers grew at each evening meeting. At first only seven congregations could come up with the necessary dues: they ranged across the spectrum of American religious life from Our Lady of Mercy Roman Catholic Church to Saint James Holiness Church and the "Church of the Divine Metaphysic." Within six months, six additional congregations had joined, including Christ Community Reformed Church and Saint Peter's Lutheran. Somehow this small group of struggling congregations managed to send thirteen people to Baltimore for ten days at the Industrial Areas Foundation Training Center.

By the beginning of 1980, the East Brooklyn Churches (EBC) Organization was clearly on its way. In January of that year eighty-five people from the neighborhood completed a twelve-hour training session in communication, research into community needs, and delegation (with accountability) of responsibilities. Later that year the group began its close association with Bishop Francis Mugavero, the Roman Catholic bishop of Brooklyn, and received his endorsement. It examined its membership, too, and proudly reported—as the minutes note—"We are Protestant and Catholic, clergy and laity, black, white, Hispanic, poor and middle-class, old and young, and all residents of the community."

Training and homework back actions

Then began, in late 1980, the string of "actions" that served notice to New York City and other local powers that something new was happening in old Brooklyn. First, EBC sent 75 people to call upon Brooklyn Borough President Howard Golden. The group packed the small meeting room so solidly that Golden had to enter alone, without his aides. The meeting was courteous, as are all EBC meetings. But it began with 20 church members serving notices of their resignations from posts on community boards and borough agencies. They could no longer serve, the members told Golden, on public bodies lacking the power or will to change conditions in Brooklyn. Then the entire group, through its spokesperson, notified the president that 1,700 street signs were down in the EBC area. They wanted them put back up, and promptly, please. Golden, it later developed, had already committed himself to replacing such signs all over the borough. This time, however, the replacement would begin in the least affluent areas. And so it did, and EBC had its first success. Note that the issue was winnable, and that EBC had known that it was.

Next the organization took up the issue of supermarkets and food stores. Members thought they observed overpricing of food in area markets; they *knew* they were seeing black lettuce and green meat; they were angry about unsanitary conditions in the markets. Nevertheless, the organization's commitment to research, and to fairness, led them to hire the head of the Manhattan Grocer's Association, a trade group, to make a survey. He came surreptitiously to Brooklyn, examined each offending market and pronounced the situation "intolerable by both industry and public standards."

As the next step in a process that has become almost standard for EBC, managers of the offending food stores were invited to a meeting. The managers need not have come, of course, but they were given to understand that absence would result in a visit by EBC folk, in force, to corporate headquarters in Manhattan or even in a more distant city. When the managers arrived they were ushered to seats facing more than 700 people. One by one, EBC members rose to recite their grievances. The excoriation was the more deadly for its calmness. Rather quickly thereafter the stores were spruced up. One merchant installed $30,000 in refrigeration equipment. Meanwhile, and for months, persons wearing large EBC badges stood near registers in targeted stores, checking prices and sanitary conditions. The "action" was controlled but nevertheless confrontational. People noticed; EBC grew; and relationships with merchants gradually became mutually respectful, culminating in 1986 when EBC helped one food store operator find capital for rebuilding after a fire.

Keep planning and say thanks

Other early EBC "actions" focussed on pressuring the city to speed up demolition of long-abandoned buildings; on forcing police and prosecutors to close so-called smoke-shops (illegal store-front operations selling narcotics); and on voter registration (EBC takes credit for registering 10,000 new voters in 1984). In each case, solid homework was done, logistical problems were solved ahead of time, initial approaches to authority were made at the highest levels, the organization's intentions or expectations were presented with clarity, and time-lines for requested actions were set. Also, when officials or bureaucrats gave good service, EBC didn't forget to say "thank you" in ways the press was bound to report. This last tactic does much to keep the organization's relationships with public officials viable, if not always warm.

Some who have come into contact with EBC "actions" have expressed distaste for their "orchestrated" character. Not Pastor Benke, however. "Nobody complains," says Benke, "when representatives of recognized power groups in our communities make 'presentations' or 'representations.' Why should they complain when ordinary people do the same?"

Strong organizations precede issues

Those familiar with community action groups in the 1960s and '70s may see two important changes in the way groups related to the IAF now operate. First, IAF-related groups do not organize around issues; they organize around churches and other solid organizations for the benefit of people in the neighborhoods. In this new style, issues become occasions for people to gain experience in empowering themselves. Then, when issues change, the organization remains.

A second difference between such groups as East Brooklyn Churches and their predecessors is found in their cold, crisp insistence on competence as a first requirement in hiring staff. Though the majority communities in Brownsville are black and Hispanic, EBC's first organizer was a white man, Mike Gecan, who gained his experience with Industrial Areas Foundation. Gecan's administrative hand was on the new organization's first steps and actions. In 1981 Gecan and EBC took on an associate, former United Farmworkers organizer Stephen Roberson, who is black. Today Roberson is the most visible EBC staff person from day to day, and he has developed inner-city organizing skills of the highest order. He originated the area network of regular house meetings where basic training and recruitment are done and people are encouraged to take on and fulfill assignments on committees and in research. During these meetings, leaders emerge. Says Roberson, "You can only demonstrate that you are a leader here; you can't just talk about it. And a leader is one whose efforts result in residual benefits for others."

Against this background of events and actions, in which more than fifty congregations are now involved and hundreds of people have gained experience in dealing with public authorities, the story of how Angel Torres got his Nehemiah house can be understood. As Saul Alinsky once said, "The relevant skill in modern urban life is that of knowing how to hold public officials accountable"—

and that is what EBC and the Nehemiah Project are all about.

A neighborhood envisions decent life

Nehemiah Homes began in the minds of East Brooklyn Churches people at a retreat in May 1981. Asked to do some dreaming, they responded with visions of good homes, good schools, shopping centers, a decent urban life. Without realizing it, they began describing what Roberson calls a "first wave assault" on rebuilding an urban neighborhood. The retreat ended with members directing Mike Gecan to develop data on housing possibilities. Mike went to (then) Lieutenant Governor Mario Cuomo for facts about mortgage possibilities. He talked with developers, investigating costs and bottlenecks. And he called on Bishop Mugavero. The bishop reported that "I told Ed Koch [mayor of New York] to build no more high-rises; to take an interest in homes." Gecan filed the bishop's remark carefully in his mind.

Then Chambers sent Gecan to see I. D. Robbins, known for his column on housing in the *Daily News*. Gecan made the long trek to New Jersey where he found a dynamo of a man already bored with semiretirement. Robbins was a seventy-five-year-old Jewish builder whose last major construction accomplishment was building a thousand homes for the New York Typographer's Union. He has stamped his name and personality on the way the Nehemiah Project does business.

Higher finance calls for strategy

Through the fall of 1981 the planning went on. EBC staff and pastors devised a scheme: the churches would raise $7.5 million, then approaches could be made to government. The pastors got busy. The Missouri Synod Lutherans, an unexpected source, expressed interest and later made a $1 million commitment to the undertaking. By now the Reverend Johnny Ray Youngblood of a local Baptist congregation had dubbed the plan "The Nehemiah Project," after the Old Testament account of the rebuilding of Jerusalem.[*]

Meanwhile, Mike Gecan ran a training session for priests who were to make an all-important approach to Bishop Mugavero. Nine of the priests, together with lay representatives, told the bishop of their plans to build two- and three-bedroom houses. He

---

[*] See the entire book of Nehemiah, a first-rate adventure story set about 450 B.C.

immediately offered $250,000. One woman exclaimed, "That's an excellent *beginning*," and they went away. Soon the bishop got back to them: "I think I can get a million." Again the response: "That's great, Bishop. Now why not go to the orders for more?" Eventually, the Roman Catholics of Brooklyn would produce $2.5 million for the project, and the Episcopalians of Long Island came up with $1 million more.

City hall is coopted as an ally

But Bishop Mugavero gave more than money: he became the EBC companion-in-arms, the arch-conspirator of them all. It was Mugavero who, as spokesperson, led the first EBC visit to Mayor Koch. In the square outside City Hall, Pastor Heinemeir led the group in prayer, and then they filed into His Honor's office. Mugavero began with a mistake: "We have raised $12 million to build homes; now we'd like $12 million from you" (actually EBC had commitments of only $7.5 million). In a familiar gesture, Koch spread his hands: "We haven't got it, Bishop; our funds are all committed." Then, as though making a great sacrifice, "We'll give you land, though." This offer was, of course, expected: the city held title to vast stretches of vacant land in East Brooklyn, and had no idea in the world what to do with it.

Again the bishop returned to the subject of money. At that moment he represented not only the Roman Catholic Diocese of Brooklyn but also, to some extent, one million New York voters of Italian descent. He said, "Ed, this is so important. There's got to be some way for you to find that money. If necessary, why don't you steal it for us?"

> Koch (laughing to his aides): "The bishop is telling me to steal it!"
> Mugavero: "If necessary, I'll give you absolution."

After three long weeks of waiting, the glad news came from the mayor. At a press conference EBC announced its intention to build 5,000 single-family row houses. Two bishops, one Lutheran treasurer, and a top representative of the mayor were present to lend credence to the promise. No wonder that Angel Torres, hearing about it, took Lydia for that drive through Brownsville.

Partners in creative complexity

The Nehemiah home-owning system is complex. The City of

New York provides land and a $10,000 no-interest loan. Mortgages come through the New York State Mortgage Agency. Removal of landfill for excavation is done at city expense, and the costs of permits and paperwork run about a third of normal rates for the area. Other savings have been made: a single sewer hookup serves multiple homes, for example, saving more than $3,000 per house.

But not everything has run smoothly. Delays in demolition have held up construction; owners of isolated lots have sometimes held out on selling, thus delaying or denying the block-long construction that is least expensive for Nehemiah's builders. Still, construction has proceeded much faster than the average for housing in New York. The rejuvenated Mother Gaston neighborhood keeps people anticipating further success. And planners did not forget to say "thank you" to Mayor Koch and to (now) Governor Cuomo when 10,000 EBC members held a huge rally in 1986.

The project battles principalities and powers

In the course of two years of construction, builder I. D. Robbins hasn't missed a day at Nehemiah Project offices. He will not admit to having fun—"a person like me owes something to the world after all," he says, "and this is serious business here. Besides, I'm getting paid." He has surrounded himself with construction workers, mostly black, whose company he obviously enjoys. I. D. has fought battle after battle with the bureaucracies—and has enjoyed them, too. It is well known that he has put a City Hall staffer on the payroll just to track necessary papers through the maze; he has done the same at the housing administration. He fought a memorable battle with the U.S. Postal Service, which barred its carriers from climbing the two steps before each Nehemiah house to slip letters into a slot in the door (letters in an outside box would have been stolen by the addicts just around the corner).

On the wall of his office, I. D. has posted a quotation from St Paul. It's the one about "principalities and powers" (Ephesians 6:12), except that "principalities" is translated as "systems." "Ed Chambers tells me that's good Greek," I. D. reports with a wink.

However, all of the "principalities and powers" of the area were not official. A gang of black criminals who more or less control the area's underworld tried to shake down contractors on the Nehemiah job and later, to secure some of the dwellings for illegal

In front of the Nehemiah Project home owned by Frederico and Blanca Blondette are Blanca (at left), three of the four Blondette children, and a cousin. The Blondettes have added the front wall and fence, a backyard patio and two finished rooms in the basement to the standard model home.

operations of one kind or another. Here too EBC's roots in the neighborhood proved useful, for I. D. Robbins told Pastor Johnny Youngblood about his problem, and Youngblood told the mothers and elderly aunts of the young gangsters about it. So the gang leaders were waited upon by a delegation much more fearsome than any the New York Police Department could ever muster and the harassment ceased.

Moving day arrives

As soon as the official announcement was made that Nehemiah construction would begin, an application bank was opened. The inexorable rule was first-come, first-served. The Torres name was high on the list, and so it was that they moved into one of the early homes. Torres tells what it felt like:

> You will think us strange, but we cried again. It was so beautiful, and our kids were so happy. In those days, at the beginning, there was no division in the backyards—no fences. The children played with the children of the new houses there. It was a new experience for them to play free. And we found that our neighbors are good people. They say "Good morning" to each other: you feel respected, and because you feel respected, you *respect back* to them. Black people and Hispanic people get along here; that part of Nehemiah is working. And most people go to church; church is part of being secure.

Churches take management role

Sooner or later it occurs to every observer of the Nehemiah Project to ask two questions:

> Who really runs things?
> What do the churches get out of it?

The answer to the first fits none of the usual assumptions about bureaucracies. The plain truth is that the *churches* run both the Nehemiah Project and EBC, and specifically, the pastors of the churches run things, together with three or four persons from each congregation. EBC has no president, for example, because it is a cooperative of congregations. It does possess, however, an informal executive committee—a clergy caucus composed of member pastors and women of religious orders. In this caucus

oungblood, the black Baptist, and Powis, the Roman Catholic
riest from Presentation Parish, "are more equal than their equals,"
; one observer notes, but no pastor of a viable congregation is
ltirely powerless.

This churchly domination bothers Angel Torres not one bit.
eports Torres, "Lydia and I take part in East Brooklyn Churches:
e are Catholics ourselves, and belong to Our Lady of Mercy
hurch. At first we were suspicious, going to other churches for
le meetings of EBC. But now it is a good experience. We don't
;k each other anymore what church we come from. We walk
l a church—any church—we feel so happy, so secure. I guess
is true that the churches run things—their leaders, I mean. But
never feel shut out. My worry instead is that I will forget how
was that first day in the new house. Or how wonderful [it is]
·hen churches have visions so great that you *have* to believe."

No one familiar with urban areas in U.S. cities should be surprised
: the continuing role of the clergy here. After all, in Brownsville
lere are no banks, civic clubs, home-office industries, or
rofessional offices—all of these have fled their responsibilities
ld gone elsewhere. Apart from the police and the rackets, the
lurches are all that remain alive in the wreckage of community.
astors of the churches of course become managers and stewards
f whatever cohesive forces remain, and therefore they hold the
ey to whatever latent, legitimate popular strength is to be found
l a burgeoning slum.

he power of money from the poor

Equally important, churches have been the only places (again
xcepting the rackets) in the area where, in recent years, earners
f marginal wages could watch capital accumulate and discover
lat the accumulated sums would be held for collective use. Even
l the Brownsville of the 1980s, the money placed in the collection
late of a large parish on Sunday can be substantial, though it
Imes from the pockets of the poor. Even small, struggling
Ingregations can accumulate at least some money for causes that
onest residents are too poor to fund themselves. Such money,
; EBC employed it, became the leverage for requesting more
loney from denominations. And that money, in turn, became the
·verage for soliciting city and state money. The power involved
. nonetheless real because it comes from small gifts prompted
y the piety of the working or hope-to-be-working poor.

Churches grow in vital neighborhood

Another benefit churches derive from EBC and the Nehemia
Project is the creation of a viable, functioning community in whic
to grow. Recently Pastor Johnny Ray Youngblood and his St. Pa
Community Baptist Church gave EBC a $100,000 interest-free loa
St. Paul's can afford the gesture. Youngblood preaches to 3,0(
or more worshipers every Sunday, a congregation growing in pa
because new people have found new homes nearby.

Eleven of the twelve Roman Catholic parishes that approache
Bishop Mugavero for help in starting Nehemiah were aid-receivin
churches. The priests promised to get their churches off subsid
if the bishop would help with Nehemiah. All but one of thes
parishes have already fulfilled that vow, in part because of th
area's new optimism, in part because through EBC, members (
black Baptist congregations visited Catholic churches to teac
stewardship. These "tithe training sessions," as Baptists call then
are astonishing encounters that, in one observer's words, "get a
theological as hell."

Even Benke's little Missouri Synod Lutheran Church ha
flourished. "In absolute terms we have increased our membershi
by only 50," the pastor says, "but deaths in our congregatior
and the continued flight of some families, made it necessary t
get 250 new members to increase by that number. We really hav
250 people here that we didn't have before. What's more, our littl
church of white, black and Hispanic people is famous all acros
the synod as 'our Brooklyn Church.' That feels good to th
members, and it feels good to me."

New strength and respect

But the biggest advantage to the churches from their work wit
East Brooklyn Churches and the Nehemiah Project is the growt
of the consciousness of strength in both pastors and people. I. [
Robbins expressed it best of all: "This church organization is s
powerful it can put 4,000 people on the streets to confront
problem, and 10,000 to deal with a mayor. The group has relate
itself closely to powerful city and state interests—to people lik
Governor Cuomo, for example, and Bishop Mugavero. While doin
these things, members of EBC have related to each other in
way that is well-nigh incredible. You can say about them tha
far from being balked by political factors, they have made ove

political conditions around here to suit themselves—that is, to fit the needs of the community. They sense this, are proud of their accomplishment, and so are happy—and unquarrelsome."

Riding home, I thought about the last words Robbins said to me: "In almost three years at Nehemiah, there has not been a single default on a mortgage." That pointed up the other benefit that churches and their pastors get from involvement in the project: deep respect for the hard-pressed people, earners of extremely modest wages, whom they seek to serve.

Since then I have often thought about that respect. Do other churches, elsewhere, truly respect their members? Respect one another? If they do, then perhaps they can unite locally across confessional lines to think the thoughts, and do the deeds, that others will not do. It requires courage to make an attempt like the Nehemiah Project. It requires a hard grasp on reality and a willingness to speak hard truth to Pharaohs and other powerful people. But it requires faith, too. And love. And the kind of respect that Angel Torres has encountered: the kind that makes you "respect back."

CONCLUSION: Breach of Promise

"You shall love the Lord your God with all your heart, and with all your soul, and with all your mind. This is the great and first commandment. And the second is like it, You shall love your neighbor as yourself. On these two commandments depend all the law and the prophets."
(Matthew 22:37)

"If you are not careful to do all the words of this law which are written in this book. . . then the Lord will bring upon you and your offspring extraordinary afflictions, afflictions severe and lasting. . . . In the morning you shall say, 'Would it were evening!' and in the evening you shall say, 'Would it were morning!' because of the dread which your heart shall fear, and the sights which your eyes shall see. And the Lord will bring you back in ships to Egypt, a journey which I promised that you should never make again. . . ."
(Deuteronomy 28:58-59, 67-68)

The people we have met in this book feel that violence has been done to them and to their families. They are not quite sure who is responsible for this violence. But they sense that certain principles, certain shared pledges, on which they should have been able to order and conduct their lives, have been violated. I think they are right, whether we look at those principles in political and economic terms or in religious and moral terms.

Origins of political promises

The two nations that share the northern 85 percent of this continent developed their political liberties down separate paths from the same source. For citizens of Canada, the path leads from the primitive beginnings of English common law to the Magna Carta and the later development in Britain of a parliamentary tradition, then onward to the British North America Act of 1867 that created the Dominion of Canada, and eventually to the repatriation of the Constitution in 1981, which meant Canada was related less closely to Britain. For citizens of the United States, the path from the same original sources diverged, beginning in 1776, to a new set of foundation documents. While continuing in the British tradition, these documents drew also from the political philosophy then developing on the European continent.

Along their shared and their divergent paths, Canadian and U.S. traditions of law and custom have brought into being on this continent—though not without fits and starts—a society of free people that in many ways transcends the border between the two countries. We Canadians and "Americans" are different from each other, yet we have much in common.

Laws and rights can be bewilderingly technical because in our nations they rest not only on basic constitutions but also on legislation, case law and layers of legal precedent. Yet these political and legal foundations, and all the changes made in them by jurists and legislators in more than three hundred years, can be summed up briefly: in our two nations we have been engaged in deciding who is a citizen, what a citizen owes to the state, what the state owes to a citizen, and what all owe to one another.

Rights of free citizens

The writers of the American Declaration of Independence

originated a phrase that captured the imaginations of people in their day and the generations that followed: ". . . all Men are created equal," they wrote (though when it came to defining citizenship, this designation was not inclusive), and "are endowed by their Creator with certain unalienable Rights, . . . among these are Life, Liberty, and the Pursuit of Happiness." This brief list has become the shorthand definition of human freedom carried in many North American heads. The phrase in itself has become a kind of "foundation document." When the rights it promises are abridged, one feels freedom's sands being washed out to sea.

The reference to "the pursuit of happiness" was not carried over to the U.S. Constitution. Instead, that sober document speaks of such matters as ensuring "domestic tranquility," establishing "justice," and promoting "the general welfare." Nevertheless, American people think they have a right to pursue happiness, and woe betide a government that ever explicitly denies that right.

When freedoms are abridged for all

In reality, all governments have understood that during times of war or civil upheaval, the state may require its citizens to put aside some freedoms for the sake of the general welfare. At such times citizens have almost always acceded to the state's demands, believing that their part in the social contract is to respond to the state's call to military service, to civil defense or to self-denial in national crises. The poor people of this book do not complain about what some of them—Margaret and Tommy Jones, Joe Siranovitch, the people of Racine or Allerton or Edgerton—suffered in World War II. And when they complain about Vietnam, their anger stems not from being asked to serve but from the fact that so many other citizens were not required to join them in that service.

When freedoms are abridged for some

When war or crisis curtails personal liberty or private pursuits, citizens generally feel that the limitations come with the territory of citizenship. But during some periods in history, freedom and that valuable "pursuit of happiness" have been abridged for other reasons: the expulsion that sent Native Americans out of the southeastern U.S. on the "Trail of Tears"; the relocation of Acadians to Louisiana; the sale and forced labor of generations of black people; the paranoid internment of Japanese-Americans during

World War II. From these events—which all led to impoverishment as well as to denial of liberty—the breaking of important, elemental principles still reverberates across our history.

I believe we are in another such period in North America. The emerging world economy—that one, huge market that ignores frontiers, separate legal traditions and freedom or its lack—makes demands of people that they do not understand, that do not fall equally on all, that do not demonstrably benefit the common welfare. (Indeed, it seems that some persons and organizations active in the world market expend great effort to ensure that a concept of common welfare across national boundaries does not have a chance to develop.)

When welfare is not common to all

As we have noted before, economic trade-offs, whether prompted by business interests or by government policy, affect jobs and livelihoods. Joe Siranovitch's job was sacrificed to a decision, made by someone somewhere, to bring in foreign steel without levying substantial import duties, in exchange for—what? The development of international conglomerates means that entire industries, towns, regions, can be abandoned like temporary campsites by great corporations in pursuit of the happiness that is measured on quarterly balance sheets. Thus, U.S. auto manufacturers close plants in Ohio, Ontario or California. They build new plants in Mexico where, under "free trade zone" arrangements, they assemble cars for export to—Ohio, Ontario or California! Canadians fear that "free trade" with the U.S. will prove costly for jobs and profits. Such economic gymnastics are too much for most of us as ordinary citizens and workers to understand. And the unemployed victims of such trade-offs, observing other countries or regions of the country thriving as a result of their deprivation, feel that their personal "pursuit of happiness" has been arbitrarily and selectively taken away—if not by direct government action, then at least as a result of government-supported policy.

The assertion that a new era is dawning for technology, service industries or international relations takes none of the sting out of what these economic decisions are doing to working people in our nations. Such new eras, often related to a nation's industrialization, have dawned before, but have done nothing to relieve the pain of the people most affected—English villagers pouring into the slums of eighteenth-century Manchester and

London, early twentieth-century southern sharecroppers pushed north to Cincinnati and Detroit, Brazilian peasants forced by expanding ranches to slash and burn ever more remote regions of rainforest to grow their food. When misfortune results not from crisis but from selective, discriminatory pauperization, and when victims perceive it as such, the victims may well conclude that a basic promise made to them by the social contract has been broken.

Messages sent to poor people

Some North Americans perceive such a breach of promise when the prevailing philosophy of businesses and governments is expressed in recurring phrases like "thinning the labor force to recover cost competitiveness" or "exporting technology to areas with lower production costs." These attitudes and practices are not new (late nineteenth-century captains of industry, for instance, were notoriously callous toward workers). What is new, at least in the United States, is to hear a director of the Federal Reserve System saying, as one did in 1985, that "a million or so Americans will be given the privilege"—through unemployment—of "helping the rest of the nation bring inflation under control."

Whether or not we have the economic expertise to understand the mechanisms to which the Federal Reserve director referred, such comments, when heard by the unemployed and other poor people, produce reactions that are summed up by Joe Siranovitch: "It just don't seem right, somehow," or by the women at Racine: "We're just hillbillies; we're not supposed to be interested in books." Such statements suggest that poor people know very well that they have been deemed of little value by the political and economic leaders of their nation. In America, poverty has always been a more-or-less temporary condition for many people, but now many who had thought that they and their children were climbing out of poverty feel themselves being plunged back in.

So the feeling is growing among poor people that their poverty has been induced or—especially for black people—prolonged by government and business decisions in which they and their welfare have been regarded as of little, or no, consequence. Since the common political beliefs in both Canada and the United States hold that neither law nor government should draw distinctions of worth between persons, there is a growing sense that a social and political contract has been breached. Thoughtful persons, I believe, will be led to admit that there is substance to these suspicions.

Religious covenants are broken

It is not only the political and economic principles and covenants by which people expect to order their lives that have been broken. Breaches in religious and moral "promises" have occurred as well. In fact, these violations of the religious and moral part of the North American social contract may well prove to be the most damaging to the future in which our nations' children will live.

To grasp the moral dimension of the broken promises that poverty represents, we need only take a long look, and a long "listen," to the sights and sounds against which millions of our North American sisters and brothers live out the experience of being poor.

Consider the background sounds in our societies. The everyday speech of successful or moderately successful people repeatedly refers to "losers"—a label to avoid at all costs. These "no-goods" are also called "parasites," "bag ladies," "welfare types," "rednecks," "bluecollar roughnecks," "dropouts," "AFDC [Aid to Families with Dependent Children] babybreeders." Conversely, we are told whom to emulate: the "winners," "achievers," "power elites," "decision makers," "Yuppies," "upwardly mobile," and so on. In reality, the differences described by these two sets of terms come down to differences in education, employment, prospects and money. But the terms assume actual distinctions of human worth between those who are "making it" and those who aren't. A simple clue is tone of voice.

Separate signals to "haves" and "have-nots"

Then consider the sights that go with being poor. Shop in Bloomingdales, Rich's or Marshall Fields. Any security measures you might notice are unobtrusive. It is assumed that you, the shopper, are honest, or at least that you have sufficient worth to deserve discretion and courtesy. Then shop in stores that in location or price are usually accessible to the poor. Signs warn you to watch your purse and to remember that these premises are surveyed by hidden cameras. The assumption—carried over from stores to restaurants to motels—is that to be poor is to be dishonest. And by today's ethic, courtesy need not be extended to those presumed to be dishonest.

Such background reminders to the poor that their quality as persons is in doubt are accompanied by real disabilities imposed willy-nilly on those least able to bear them. For example, in assuming that "everyone" owns a car, North American cities and counties save money by cutting back on public transportation. Never mind that the poor must walk long distances to work or shop, or be forced to buy a car and try to keep it running. And because many wages, assets and hospital costs are high these days, so are judgments awarded in auto accident cases, raising the cost of auto insurance. As a result, poor people (who may live where insurance rates are highest), have to pay premiums that consume a high proportion of their incomes in order to travel even to low-paying jobs.

Or consider the effect that the growth in high technology has on those who lack skills for "high-tech" jobs. Industries requiring these skills have brought engineers, chemists and computer experts to small, "blue-collar" towns near Boston, Pittsburgh, Newark, San Diego and other large cities. Older than the suburban communities between themselves and the cities, these small towns have been places where working people could buy a home for a modest sum or rent an apartment reasonably. Now modest wage-earners are being forced out of homes and apartments by rising taxes and the pressures of so-called gentrification. Many of these displaced persons have no place else to go. Low and even moderate income housing isn't being built. If a job is lost, an entire family may find itself living in the street. These families live in cars, sleep in parks, wander in confusion from one rumor of employment to another. Sometimes, children of the more comfortable, having heard their elders talk about "homeless bums," react with violence to the vagrants. Not too long ago in a large U.S. city, gasoline was poured over a couple sleeping in the street and they were set on fire.

Witnesses to the experience of poverty

When we begin to see what life in North America looks like from the perspective of the poor, when we notice whose faces are left out of the pervasive pictures of "the good life," when we hear what is said about the worth of people and the tone in which it is spoken, when we listen for the silence of those deemed not worthy of speaking for themselves, then we become witnesses.

But the act of bearing witness to these sights and sounds is not pleasant. It puts us in an uncomfortable tension with ourselves, with our desires for a comfortable life and with a society that likes to think itself postive and productive. Our position is like that of a driver who sees the car up ahead crash. The driver becomes a witness to who was at fault and, in speaking about what was seen, is forced to keep replaying a mental image of the horror. But long before the driver gets to court to testify, he or she must make a snap decision about whether or not to stop and help, and whether to register his or her presence as a witness or to drive on to a personal destination.

Witnesses to the promises of faith

If, by hearing accounts of those who cope with poverty or by examining our attitudes toward poverty, we become witnesses to gaps in the social fabric, to the injustice that so quickly finds new forms of expression, then how do we affirm at the same time our witness to the gospel of Jesus Christ? How shall we bear witness both to what befalls the poor and to the one who came to "preach good news to the poor"? The decision to hear with both ears, to see with both eyes, to let our reality be set in the light of God's reality, stretches us painfully; it is, I think, one way we are called to "take up our cross" and follow Jesus. If we let go of the uncomfortable reality of those who live in poverty in our midst, we risk failing to be witnesses to the gospel, because we miss seeing the Christ who came to live as a poor person among the poor.

When we contrast present attitudes toward poor people with the biblical witness we have been taught in our churches, we feel that something has happened to us, something ugly, while we were not watching or listening. I don't want to convey a nostalgic yearning for the "golden age" of North America. To be poor one or two hundred years ago on this continent was not an enviable position. There were few pension plans, no public old-age benefits; to organize a union was dangerous if not unheard-of; the risk of disease or accident was greater. Distinctions of race, sex, and social class were upheld: some people were slaves, some were indentured servants, some were women without rights to their own earnings. No one in these groups could vote, and many could not read and write.

Yet, looking back, there seems to have been more respect for working people. Now when a job is lost, the person becomes a "loser," with all the negative connotations attached. Once we would have admired a woman like Jean (Chapter Six), who would not be forced from her home when her child needed her; now she is castigated as a "welfare mother." It is as if our societies had determined sometime, somewhere, that the elemental human functions—earning bread no matter how humble the job, nurturing children no matter how modest the dwelling—are beneath our human dignity. If we talk this way for long, we shall soon believe what we say.

Once we lived with more reminders of the humble origins we all share. "A wandering Aramaean was my father," the line spoken for centuries in Jewish households, held much meaning in North America one or two generations ago, when many knew themselves to be children or grandchildren of immigrants, most of whom were poor. Our immigrant heritage recalled the biblical patterns we were taught. In churches the story of the escape of a group of slaves from Egypt was told and retold. This tradition was particularly precious to those who lived as slaves in America. But Moses, Aaron, Miriam, Joshua, the names of those who led the Hebrew people in their wilderness wanderings, lived in the imaginations of all of us and in the names given to our children. To be rootless, without resources, searching for a home, was not disgraceful, because a great many people were doing and had done it. We called it "pioneering," and later, "nation-building."

Biblical witness to the poor among us

The biblical teaching we received went further than respect for the wanderers of history. As passages of Scripture throughout this book make clear, the Bible pictures a shalom community in which the poor are to be considered part of the people. Thus the community as a whole will bear witness to God's good purpose. The membership of the poor in the community gives them rights— to glean in fields and vineyards, to approach rulers and magistrates. Whether we were listening or not, the Scriptures read to us indicated that when the grievances of the poor are not set right, those who have failed to serve justice will be penalized.

The poor who belong to the community along with everyone else must, the Old Testament insists, be served in their need by those who are more comfortably placed. By this ethic, the poor should not have to ask for help; the community should see that they are relieved of distress. Thus the vision of a seventh year when debts and bondage are cancelled has haunted the Judeo-Christian tradition as it is understood in North America. The New Testament parables of the feast to which all are invited, with the poor brought from the highways and byways, presents a vision of the future that God desires and the hope that Christians witness to.

The teaching that has formed our faith also includes Jesus' version of the ancient question about the place of the poor: "Who is my neighbor?" The concept of the community as a restricted clan or tribe, as the group of "those who matter" in village or city, can never be accepted again. The perimeters of caring have pushed outward from the circle of the family and the nation.

Sorting out our loyalties

However well or poorly we have understood and practiced these teachings, we sense that they are ideals that have shaped us as Christians and in many ways have shaped our nations as well. Certainly, we have learned that nations, especially those that honor freedom of religion and value cultural and ethnic diversity, are not specifically Christian entities. And we have learned that it is dangerous when a modern nation considers itself to be *"the* people of God." Yet from the beginning we have felt that in our national lives we were acting on high religious principles. We expect our national policies and actions to be clothed in the language of service, community and justice. Whatever the origin of secular laws in the United States and Canada, it is certainly true that in our national myths we have seen ourselves as people seeking to live and act under God and under God's laws. So we are disappointed when our nation does not live up to ideals that have been derived principally from Judeo-Christian traditions.

Much religious discourse, agony and antipathy in this century have arisen from thorny questions about the loyalties of Christians to Jesus Christ and to their nations (of course, similar issues also arise among other communities of faith). These questions of allegiance have been especially controversial for North Americans because, as we have noted, the ideals concerning our nation are so intertwined with the biblical principles of our faith. So when promises—to create a society that includes everyone, to guarantee the rights and care for the lives of those among us who have the least—are broken across a nation, when does Christian witness begin to speak out? Where does Christian witness, which never limits itself to neutral observation, begin to heal?

When it comes to ordering our loyalties, we must sometimes strive for balance, sometimes let our passion for justice and mercy carry us into action. Even if we knew how, we could not compel a nation to accept a Christian interpretation of the basic promises regarding community or to fulfill those promises from Christian motives. Yet we have understood our commitment to freedom, justice and liberty to be the expression in public action of all that we have been taught by faith.

Christian witness in pluralistic nations

My approach comes down to witnessing. Witnessing as Christians to the love and justice we know in Jesus Christ. Witnessing by recalling a nation to its own ideals of justice, as we are led by the Spirit to understand justice. Witnessing to the realities in the lives of the poor. Witnessing to respect for self-determination and to compassion in all our efforts to let the poor have the say in their future, and thereby witnessing to the need to restore those qualities to our public assistance programs—many of which began as campaigns by religious people to address problems of poverty. And most importantly, witnessing to the ultimate powerlessness of power that seeks its own gain and to the power of powerlessness in Jesus Christ, who humbled himself to serve, who made himself poor that we might be rich (Philippians 2:7-8; II Corinthians 8:9).

The temptations of money

As we continue to witness by standing in community with the poor, we will encounter crosscurrents that may sweep us in other directions. One strong pull is a prevailing attitude toward money— how it is gotten, kept and used. That attitude is summed up by the slogan and contents of a newspaper that bills itself as "the daily diary of the American dream." This "diary" reports the day-to-day rise and fall of markets, stock prices and other investments, wrapping the whole in articles about who is up and who is down, who is rich and who has gone broke in the commercial arena. But the attitude goes far beyond the stance of a particular newspaper, for this redefinition of "the" American dream pervades the lives of many without funds to invest, many whose credit is already overdrawn by purchases of the consumer items regarded as essential to "the good life."

The ethical challenge set by economic power or by a completely economic view of life is not new, but it seems to have intensified in recent years. Economic betterment has always been part of the American aspiration; in fact, in this book we have been talking about economic betterment for many North Americans. The poor are poor precisely because they lack money. So the question put to our commitment is not about money in itself but about principles, about highest loyalties and about the definition of the happiness that we have the right to pursue. Each of us knows how easily our Christian witness is sidetracked by this economic "dream." How shall we shape our own lives, our spending patterns, our church budgets, amid the pull of this current? How shall we witness to God's purpose in societies that claim to be founded on dignity, liberty, justice—yet seem to be run by the power of money?

The temptations of national security

Another crosscurrent, one that is especially strong in the United States, is the claim that our highest national priority must be security—preserving "the American way of life" through strength. We all want strong nations—but how will we define that strength? Often, "security" is used as a synonym for "military strength." There have been times, I think, when security defined in military terms has rightly been given high national priority. But right now, I believe it is time for the need for military security as the national priority to give way in great measure to the needs of the poor, the unemployed and the underemployed, both for mercy's sake and for the well-being of our republics. The people's trust teeters on a dangerous edge, endangering confidence not only in a nation's political leadership but in its ideals as well. The integrity of all parties and groups, the ideals that bind us together as a people, are at stake.

As Christians, we must witness to what we mean by strength. Can a heavily armed nation be strong when children are its poorest people, as is true in the United States? When those who understand and cherish its farmlands are forced to leave them? When the number of people who must turn for the barest subsistence to church or community food pantries keeps growing? When forty percent of those who work earn less than is required to support a family (less than $11,000 in the U.S.)? What does it mean to be a nation that is strong for the present and the future?

A time for defense—of the poor

An incident from the Bible can help us with these definitions of strength. In 445 B.C., Jerusalem lies in ruins, its wall torn down, its gates destroyed. The popular leader, Nehemiah, presses the people to rebuild the walls even as enemy troops gather outside the half-repaired citadel. Every person labors at the mission of security: half stand guard, half work on the wall, weapons in hand. Meanwhile, every sunrise reveals more enemy ranks massing on the hillsides.

Suddenly the work is interrupted. A delegation, complaining bitterly, approaches Nehemiah. The poor people of the town have come to say, in effect, "We are going broke; please help us." Far from dismissing them with a "guns before butter" speech, Nehemiah takes time to investigate and discovers that people are indeed being "ripped off" by city officials and nobles.

Immediately Nehemiah suspends all work and convenes a huge meeting. There he excoriates the corrupt leaders, forces them to cancel the poor people's debts and to give back their land, and elicits legal oaths not to repeat the offense. Only then do the citizens go back to building the wall (Nehemiah 5:1-13).

A time to restore justice

We do not live in a half-built country town besieged by nomadic raiders. We are citizens of two "developed" nations, part of a community of nations confronting another great nation and its community in what often appears to be a race for power and supremacy. We live in a time of danger from our opponents— and from ourselves. Here we must bear witness as followers of Jesus Christ. I believe we also live in a time when we can see in the faces and hear in the voices of the poor people in our midst what Nehemiah saw and heard when he met with his city's poor. It is time for us also to put justice first for those among us who are poor, a time to stand back from the walls a while to help some of our brothers and sisters to recover, a time to put down the weapons and restore the rights of the dispossessed in the land.

Our faith teaches that God is just. Late or soon, with our initiative or without it, God's justice will indeed "roll down like waters, and righteousness like an ever-flowing stream." When that time comes, when, as Mary sang, those of low degree will be exalted,

hope that you and I and the church of which we are a part
will appear in God's eyes as faithful witnesses to the enveloping
flood of mercy rather than as part of the number left high and
dry for their hardness of heart.

I hope that Christian citizens of Canada and the United States
choose to act on the mutual indebtedness inherited from our
mothers and fathers, by reclaiming for ourselves a sense of shared
identity with all who are poor or strangers or homeless, and by
taking for ourselves and our posterity possession of an ancient
promise:

> "If you pour yourself out for the hungry
>   and satisfy the desire of the afflicted,
> then shall your light rise in the darkness
>   and your gloom be as the noonday. . . .
> And your ancient ruins shall be rebuilt;
>   you shall raise up the foundations of many generations;
> you shall be called the repairer of the breach,
>   the restorer of streets to dwell in."
> (Isaiah 58:10, 12)

APPENDIX

Additional materials and sources for information are listed in the bibliography and filmography in the study guide to this book, *Keeping Covenant with the Poor* (see the inside back cover). Useful studies and statements on poverty and economic conditions have been issued by many denominations.

INTRODUCTION: The Poor in the Land

Biblical and theological considerations of poverty:

Who Are the Poor? The Beatitudes as a Call to Community, by John S. Pobee. Geneva: World Council of Churches Publications, 1987. An African theologian examines Jesus' teachings as well as his dealings with the poor (and the rich), with helpful conclusions about the church's ministry.

Jesus, Liberation and the Biblical Jubilee: Images For Ethics and Christology, by Sharon Ringe. Philadelphia: Fortress Press, 1985. Ways of understanding and applying God's directives about the years of release and restoration.

The Land, by Walter Brueggemann. Philadelphia: Fortress Press, 1982. A biblical look at "the earth" and "the land"—and questions of ownership, occupancy and power.

PART I: Portraits of Poverty
Chapter 1: Monongahela's Widow Jones

The fastest growing age group in the U.S. is made up of persons who, like Margaret Jones, are over 65. The percentage of older adults in the population is expected to grow from about 12 percent at present to 22 percent by the year 2050. Expanded Social Security and related benefits have helped decrease poverty among the elderly in the last 20 years. But poverty and economic vulnerability remain more widespread among the elderly than among other adult groups, especially for women, members of minorities, those living alone and those over 85. U.S. "poverty lines," as defined by the Census Bureau, are set lower for the elderly than for other age groups: $5,156 for an individual, $6,503 for a couple in 1985. If poverty level criteria were consistent, as it is in Canada's figures (where it is also much higher—see footnote on page 10), the poverty rate among the elderly would increase substantially.

The income support system for elderly Canadians has three major components: Old Age Security/Guaranteed Income Supplement Program (corresponding to Social Security and SSI); the Canada and Quebec Pension Plans (a mandatory plan for contributions by employers and employees); and private pensions and savings. In 1986, 2.6 million Canadians received OAS payments; about one-half of these received partial or maximum GIS benefits (the maximum total combination was $7,490). About half the total elderly population received C and Q pension benefits in 1985. In these plans, as well as in private plans, a much smaller percentage of women are recipients, because most women have worked fewer years and for lower pay. For further information:

Why Survive? Being Old in America, by Robert N. Butler. New York: Harper & Row, 1975, 1985.

"On the Other Side of Easy Street," a 1987 report of the Villers Foundation (1334 G. Street, N.W., Washington, DC 20005). Short but comprehensive presentation of the "myths and facts about the economics of old age."

The National Council on Aging, 600 Maryland Ave., S.W., Westwing 100, Washington, DC 20024.

The National Interfaith Coalition on Aging, 298 South Hull St., P.O. Box 1928, Athens, GA 30363.

"Retirement Income Programs in Canada," by Hubert Frenken, in the Winter 1986 issue of *Canadian Social Trends*, a quarterly magazine published by Statistics Canada, Publication Sales, Ottawa, Ont. KlA OT6, Canada. Single issues, $12.50 in Canada, $15 elsewhere (check with a college library or Canadian consulate for issues of this magazine in the U.S.). The Winter 1986 issue also has articles on conditions of registered Indians, the decline of real family income, and children in low-income families.

Chapter 2: Joe Siranovitch Reflects

In addition to being older Americans, Joe and Liz Siranovitch are among the millions of North Americans affected by the related problems of the movement of industry, especially "heavy" or goods-producing industry, to other areas of the nation or beyond national borders. Although U.S. and Canadian unemployment has been decreasing, many new jobs are in retail sales, maintenance, and food service, which often pay low wages and offer (in the U.S.) few or no benefits. According to a Joint Economic Committee report, an estimated 44 percent of the new jobs created in the U.S. between 1979 and 1985 paid less than $7,400 a year. When industries close or move, workers must often settle for these lower-paying service sector jobs. Similar situations affect Canadian workers, especially in one-industry (mining, paper) and old manufacturing industry (textiles, tires) areas. Regions that lose these manufacturing jobs often do not attract even the lower-paying service jobs. For more information:

"The Working Poor," by Mary Anderson Cooper, in *Seeds*, August 1987. Seeds is a network of Christians concerned about hunger: 222 East Lake Drive, Decatur, GA 30030. Magazine is $16 a year, $1 for back issues.

The New American Poverty, by Michael Harrington. New York: Penguin Books, 1985. Deals with unemployed blue-collar workers and many other groups experiencing poverty; advocates changes in government policies.

"Annual Review of Labour Force Trends" in *Canadian Social Trends* (see section on Chapter 1), in the Autumn 1986 and 1987 issues. Spring 1987 issue has articles on the changing industrial mix of employment and increases in long-term unemployment.

"No Escape: The Minimum Wage and Poverty," by Isaac Shapiro. June 1987 report available for $4 from Center on Budget and Policy Priorities, 236 Massachusetts Ave., N.E., Suite 305, Washington, DC 20002.

Chapter 3: Racine Revisited

The people of Racine live with economic problems that have plagued Appalachian and coal mining communities for at least a century. Other regions of North America also face long-term regional economic problems, as do workers employed by industries that depend on a region's natural resources—logging, fishing, copper mining and others. Miners—whether in Canada, the U.S., England, South Africa or elsewhere—have long endured a precarious physical and economic existence.

Two difficulties that people in Racine share with many others, regardless of region, are lack of housing and increased hunger. Homelessness is higher in urban areas, but lack of affordable housing as well as doubled-up and substandard housing are prevalent in small towns and rural areas also. In the U.S., members of families with children represent an estimated 28 to 40 percent of the homeless. In Charleston, the West Virginia city nearest to Racine, for example, such families make up 30 to 50 percent of the homeless. Costs of housing have been rising far faster than have incomes of renters (and the real values of incomes have been decreasing). Since 1981, U.S. government-assisted funds for low-income housing have been cut 75 percent. See section on Chapter 9 for further information.

The Physician Task Force on Hunger in America estimated that in 1985 about 20 million people in the U.S., including 12 million children, were hungry at some point each month. Between 1982 and '85, the federal food stamp program was cut by $6.8 billion, pushing several hundred thousand people out of the program and reducing benefits to millions. The Thrifty Food Plan, on which food stamp allotments are based, has inadequate, unrealistic nutritional and cost standards for many families, according to some nutritionists. The federal "poverty level" is set by tripling the cost of the Thrifty Food Plan. In West Virginia, the food stamp allotment is comparatively high, but Aid to Families with Dependent Children (AFDC or "welfare") allotments are comparatively low. In 1985, the combined total was $6,156 a year for a family of four. The federal poverty level for such a family that year was $10,609. For more information:

Hunger in America: The Growing Epidemic, published by the Physician Task Force on Hunger in America. Middletown, Conn.: Wesleyan University Press, 1985 (distributed by Harper & Row). Some of the figures above come from the Task Force's report, "Hunger Counties 1986."

Life, Work and Rebellion in the Coal Fields: The Southern West Virginia Miners, by David Alan Corbin. Champaign: University of Illinois Press, 1980.

The Commission on Religion in Appalachia (CORA), P.O. Box 10867,

Knoxville, TN 37939-0867.

Chapter 4: Molly's Salary

Statistically, elderly black women who live alone—like Molly—are among the most economically deprived groups in U.S. society. In this grouping of people, 54.5 percent are poor. The author's point is that Molly is *not* regarded by her community as a statistic, but as a unique person with much to give. Yet to be old, to be female, to be black or Hispanic, and to live alone all add to the likelihood of poverty (see "On the Other Side of Easy Street", in section on Chapter 1). In addition, until relatively recently, employers of domestic workers were not required to contribute to Social Security for their employees (much less provide other benefits).

The relation of race to poverty is an ongoing issue in the United States, as in many countries. While most U.S. people who are poor are white, the percentage of white people who are poor is lower. In 1985, whites were 84.8 percent of the population; their poverty rate was 11 percent. The poverty rate among blacks, who are 12.1 percent of the population, was 31.1 percent; among Hispanics, who were 7.9 percent of the population, the poverty rate was 27.3 percent. Historical and continuing prejudice are among the reasons for this disparity; recent studies deal with these as well as more narrowly "economic" factors, usually focussing on the urban black community. For further reflection, see the special session on Racism and Poverty in the study guide, *Keeping Covenant with the Poor.*

The Truly Disadvantaged: The Inner City, the Underclass and Public Policy, by William Julius Wilson. Illinois: University of Chicago Press, 1987. This is one of the studies referred to above; it deals with unemployment, loss of manufacturing, racism, and the changing urban community.

The National Caucus and Center on Black Aged, Inc., 1424 K Street, N.W., Suite 500, Washington, DC 20005.

Chapter 5: John and Jane Farmer Plant a Cross

For further information on the farm crisis:

The Family Farm: Can It Be Saved? by Shantilal P. Bhagat. Elgin, Ill.: Brethren Press, 1985. Overview of history, current conditions and economics, and future of agriculture in the U.S., with a theological perspective. ($2.95 postpaid from Brethren Press, 1451 Dundee Ave., Elgin, IL 60120).

Down to Earth: The Crisis in Canadian Farming, by Carol Giangrande. Toronto: Anansi, 1985.

"Rural Crisis: A Call for Justice and Action," by the Rural Crisis Issue Team, NCC, 1985. Statements of farm crisis issues and the churches' responses at regional, national and ecumenical levels. $5 (includes postage) from Domestic Hunger and Povety Project, National Council of Churches Division of Church and Society, Room 572, 475 Riverside Drive, New York, NY 10115.

Center for Rural Affairs, P.O. Box 405, Walthill, NE 60867. Deals with issues of public policy in the decline of family farms; publishes guides on public policies and a monthly newsletter, "Small Farm Advocate."

Federation of Southern Cooperatives and Land Assistance Fund, 100 Edgewood Ave., S.E., Atlanta, GA 30303. Training and technical assistance for farming cooperatives and a revolving loan fund.

Prairiefire: The Farm Crisis Project, 550 11th Street, Suite 200, Des Moines, IA 50309. Works to keep small and medium sized family farms in operation; provides technical and legal counsel to farmers.

Rural Advancement Fund/National Sharecroppers Fund, 2124 Commonwealth Ave., Charlotte, NC 28205. Have addressed the problems of agriculture and low-income rural people for 45 years.

Chapter 6: A Hard Life in "The Corridor"

In both Canada and the U.S., women are signficantly poorer than men. Increasingly larger percentages of the poor are women—and the children they are responsible for. In the U.S. in 1986, 34.6 percent of all families headed by women were poor; for black families headed by women, the rate was 50.2 percent; for Hispanic families, 51.2 percent; for white families, 28.2 percent. In Canada in 1984, the rate of poverty among female-headed, single-parent families was 47.7 percent. In that same year, over two-thirds of all children living with only their mother were in low-income families (the Canadian low-income cut-offs do not necessariy equate with poverty). In 1985, 1.1 million Canadian children (19 percent) lived in families with low incomes. In the U.S., over 13 million children were poor in 1987.

Some reasons for the increase: more households are headed by women; women earn less money than men although an increasing number of women are employed (the wage gap is narrowing, in part because men are earning less as industrial jobs decline); the lack of good child care at reasonable cost; and, especially in the U.S., mothers who work at low-paying jobs tend to lose medical and other welfare benefits for their children. The welfare system itself tends to separate families—families with an adult male present have difficulty qualifying for AFDC. See:

Women and Poverty in America, edited by Rochelle Lefkowitz and Ann Withorn. New York, Pilgrim Press, 1987. This and the next book combine accounts of women in situations of poverty with social analysis.

Women and Children Last: The Plight of Poor Women in Affluent America, by Ruth Sidel. New York: Viking Press, 1986.

Families in Peril: An Agenda for Social Change, by Marian Wright Edelman. Cambridge, Mass.: Harvard University Press, 1987. Analysis of problems of poor black and white families, preventative strategies and policy change.

The Children's Defense Fund, 122 C. Street, Washington, DC 20001. Ms. Edelman (see last entry) is president of this organization that supplies excellent analyses and other resources on the economic problems of U.S. children, including "A Children's Defense Budget: An Analysis of the Federal Year [current year] Budget and Children," and "Black and White

Children in America—Key Facts" (1985).

Chapter 7: Falling Through the Net

Feelings of anger, helplessness, despair and guilt are experienced by many people who lose their jobs. Job loss and difficulty finding new employment affect physical and emotional health. An excellent, readable study is *Unemployment: Its Impact on Body and Soul: Questions and Answers Addressing the Human Costs of Unemployment*, prepared by Sharon Kirsh for the Canadian Mental Health Association. Available in English and French for $10 (Can.) from the Association's National Office, 2160 Young St., Toronto, Ont. M4S 2Z3, Canada.

Many reasons for (and results of) unemployment are common to Canada and the U.S., but Canada's unemployment rate is higher. Much Canadian industry is controlled by foreign investors; much capital equipment and goods are imported, while raw materials and natural resources are exported; more Canadian industry is seasonal (see section on Chapter 2).

An issue related to poverty raised in this and other chapters is the cost of health care. In the U.S., private health care and health insurance are the the rule. Health insurance is offered as a benefit by many employers or unions; low-paying service-sector jobs usually lack this benefit. Private policies are quite expensive. To obtain public health care through Medicaid one must (depending on the state that administers it) have income low enough to qualify for welfare (which means that assets, such as home ownership are severely restricted). In 1986, Medicaid covered only 42 percent of all poor families. If one is unemployed, in transit or an illegal alien, often there is no health care or protection at all.

Publicly funded health care has been developed over the last 30 years in Canada. Services are a primary responsibility of the provinces; the federal government formulates national standards, assists in financing provincial programs and provides health services to native peoples. Canadians pay for provincial plan insurance through their employment or as individuals. Assistance in paying part or all of the premium is available to low-income persons; coverage for those over 65 is free. Medical and hospital care are covered; some assistance for prescriptions is available. Almost all legal residents are eligible to obtain insurance. See:

"National Health Insurance: Canada and the U.S.," a brochure with five articles by Maureen Law and Melvin Glasser; 25 cents from Health Security Action Council, 1757 N Street, Washington, DC 20036.

Chapter 8: The Criminal Dimension

"Despite the lack of statistical [profiles on prisoners], most Canadians have a fairly good sense of who prisoners are. Social workers say that many prisoners were foster children. A brief glance at any prison visiting room is enough to establish that prisoners and their families are not usually from the affluent parts of town.

". . .The biases built into the justice system create cushions for well-off offenders, protections which are not available to the resourceless. A highly skilled and well paid lawyer. . . a well-dressed, consistently employed and comfortably housed defendant will probably make a good impression on a court" (from ISSUE 29; see below).

These observations on criminal offenders hold true for the U.S. as well. It is also true that those who are poorest are most likely to be victims of crime. A U.S. Government Report to the Nation on Crime and Violence (1983) noted that rates "Violent crime rates are highest for lower-income people. Theft rates are highest for people with low incomes (less than $3,000 a year) and those with high incomes (more than $25,000)." See:

The Rich Get Richer and the Poor Get Prison: Ideology, Class, and Criminal Justice, by Jeffrey K. Reiman. New York: John Wiley and Sons, 1979. Looks at biases basic to criminal justice system, offers recommendations.

Women in Jail and Prison: A Training Manual for Volunteer Advocates. Written by Constance Baugh for the NCC Justice for Women Working Group. Comprehensive notebook with sections on theology, on history and present operation of criminal justice system, women offenders, preparation for advocacy, resource listings. Good listing of organizations. $9 from National Council of Churches Division of Church and Society, Room 572, 475 Riverside Drive, New York, NY 10115.

"Crime and Justice: Toward Rebuilding Community," ISSUE 29 (Jan. 1984). ISSUEs offer critical assessments of social concerns in Canada from Christian perspective; each ISSUE deals with a different concern. Single copies, 40 cents plus postage, from Office of Church in Society, Division of Mission in Canada, 85 St. Clair Ave. E., Toronto, Ont. M4T lM8 Canada.

Chapter 9: The Lost Indian

For sources of information about health insurance, health care and poverty, see the Appendix section on Chapter 7. Other concerns from this chapter could lead to further research in several areas.

New Testament Hospitality: Partnership with Strangers as Promise and Mission, by John Koenig. Philadelphia: Fortress Press, 1985.

The Faces of Homelessness, by Marjorie Hope and James Young. Toronto, Ont. and Lexington, Mass.: Lexington Books, D.C. Heath and Co., 1986. Analysis of U.S. welfare system and the ways it hampers efforts to help the homeless; projects and programs with the homeless.

"No Fixed Address: International Year of Shelter for the Homeless," is the theme of the March/April issue of *Perception: A Canadian Magazine of Social Concern.* Articles in English and French on issues of homelessness and housing in Canada. This bi-monthly magazine ($18 Canadian, $23 U.S. a year) and other useful resources are published by the Canadian Council on Social Development, a national non-profit organization: 55 Parkdale Ave., Ottawa, Ont. K1Y 4G1, Canada.

Stories of Survival: Conversations with Native Americans, edited by Remmelt and Kathleen Hummelen. New York, Friendship Press, 1985. Threats to cultural survival for this continent's first peoples have included threats of poverty, joblessness, isolation, poor health.

"The Socio-Demographic Conditions of Registered Indians," by Andrew J. Siggner, *Canadian Social Trends*, Winter 1986 (see section on Chapter 1).

Ministry of the Dispossessed, by Pat Hoffman. Los Angeles: Wallace Press, 1987. Interviews and accounts of farm workers in California and the churches' involvement in migrant ministry.

Health for the Nation's Harvesters: A History of the Migrant Health Program in its Economic and Social Setting, by Helen L. Johnston. Farmington Hills, Mich.: Migrant Worker Health Council, 1985 (29000 Eleven Mile Road, Farmington Hills, MI 48018). A thorough look at conditions in which migrants and seasonal farmworkers live and labor.

PART III: Face to Face, Hand to Hand
Chapter 10: What a Church Can Do

The most pertinent research on church action to alleviate poverty will take place in your own community. Almost all localities in the U.S. and Canada, whatever the population, will have churches and church members involved in such action as groups or as individuals. In addition to the kind of sources suggested in Chapter 10, do basic research at local government and social service agencies on the population mix, income levels, employment, housing, visible and hidden needs.

For statistical background about U.S. government poverty programs and suggestions for becoming an advocate for those programs, consult the resource packet, "Hunger Action Agenda: 1987 and Beyond," $2.50 from the Domestic Hunger and Poverty Project, National Council of Churches (for address, see section on Chapter 5).

A discussion of the adequacy of and advocacy for some Canadian programs is in *Food Banks and the Welfare Crisis*, by Graham Riches. Ottawa: Canadian Council on Social Development, 1986 (see section on Chapter 9).

Pennsylvania Prison Society, 311 S. Juniper Street, Philadelphia, PA 19107. Monitors prisons, provides assistance to prisoners and families, encourages alternatives to prison. For other organizations, see *Women in Jail and Prison* manual in section on Chapter 8.

Chapter 11: Straw for the Bricks of Brooklyn

An article in the *New York Times* (Sunday, Sept. 27, 1987, real estate section) on the Nehemiah project stresses the value of the project, then notes some problems in replicating it: acquiring the large blocks of cleared land necessary to make the model cost-effective means some "slum clearance," with its long-recognized human problems; and the cost of these houses, though low, is still too high for a large part of the city's population.

For other ventures into community organizing and construction of low-cost housing, consult:

Project ACTS, the Association of Churches for Training and Service, 20 Como Road, Readville, MA 02137. An ecumenical, community organzing and evangelism of eight South Boston Churches has won over $4 million in public and private funds for community improvements. and is now working to build 320 units of elderly, affordable family and market-rate housing in a former railyard.

Habitat for Humanity, Inc., Habitat and Church Streets, Americus, GA 31709. Habitat, which involves volunteers along with poor families who are potential owners in building and rehabilitating housing, gained national publicity through the involvement of former U.S. president Jimmy Carter. Groups are organized in a number of urban and rural communities (and in some other nations).

CONCLUSION : Breach of Promise

The Predicament of the Prosperous, by Bruce C. Birch and Larry L. Rasmussen. Philadelphia: Westminster Press, 1978.

Equality, by William Ryan. New York: Pantheon Books, 1981. A thoughtful account of inequality in the U.S., looking at the contradictions between rhetoric and reality.

From Poor Law to Welfare State: A History of Social Welfare in America, Third Edition, by Walter Trattner. New York: Free Press, 1984.

"Smaller Slices of the Pie: The Growing Economic Vulnerability of Poor and Moderate Income Americans," prepared by the Center on Budget and Policy Priorities, Nov. 1985 (236 Massachusetts Ave., N.E., Suite 305, Washington, DC 20002; ask for a publications list).

Poverty in Canada, by Dennis Drainville. Toronto: Anglican Book Centre, 1983.

"The Church and the Economic Crisis," the policy of the United Church of Canada, based on action taken by the 30th General Council, 1985. Single copies, 10 cents, from National Working Group on the Economy and Poverty, Division of Mission in Canada, 85 St. Clair Ave. E., Toronto, Ont. M4T lM8, Canada. Useful in itself and a reminder to consult other Canadian and U.S. denominations for appropriate statements and studies.

Appendix prepared by Carol Ames with thanks to Liz Mellon, Nancy Carter and Mary Ellen Lloyd.